THE CIVIC GUARD
MUTINY

Brian McCarthy

MERCIER PRESS

IRISH PUBLISHER – IRISH STORY

MERCIER PRESS

Cork

www.mercierpress.ie

© Brian McCarthy, 2012

ISBN: 978 1 78117 045 8

10 9 8 7 6 5 4 3 2 1

A CIP record for this title is available from the British Library

Printed and bound in the EU.

Front cover (bottom) image: *Assistant Commissioner Patrick Brennan TD, in the driver's seat of a Wolseley Stellite motor car, which he received in September 1922 as a token of gratitude from the recruits of Kildare Barracks. Courtesy of the Garda Museum and Archives.*

Back cover image: *A group of the earliest Civic Guard recruits in the RDS, Ballsbridge. Courtesy of the Garda Museum and Archives.*

CONTENTS

In memory of my uncle,
William F. (Liam) McCarthy (1934–2010)

Acknowledgements

The publication of this book is largely due to the encouragement and support of Dr Deirdre Raftery, under whose guidance and direction I previously completed a PhD on the history of the education and training of recruits in the Garda Síochána at University College Dublin. I also wish to acknowledge the assistance of Professor Mary Daly under whose supervision I completed an MA in 20th Century Irish Studies at University College Dublin in 1996. I am grateful to the staffs of the UCD School of Education, National Archives of Ireland and National Library of Ireland. Since 1994 I have been a regular visitor to the Garda Museum and Archives, and have had the pleasure of meeting a staff who always facilitate the researcher in a hospitable and professional manner. In particular, I wish to acknowledge the assistance of retired Inspector John Duffy, whose passion for police history has been a source of inspiration to my research. I wish to express my appreciation to the author Pádraig Óg Ó Ruairc for his generosity in sharing sources and responding to my many historical queries relating to County Clare. Thanks is also due to Joe Humphreys for his advice and encouragement, and to my colleague Seán Ruane, who provided suggestions and perspectives that proved invaluable.

I wish to sincerely thank Mary Feehan and the staff at

Mercier Press for all their efforts in assisting me in the completion of this book.

On a personal note, I owe my wife Karen enormous and inexpressible thanks for yet again displaying endless patience, tolerance and support. I must especially thank my parents, Brian and Nancy, and my wider family and friends, for all their assistance and encouragement throughout the completion of this book.

PROLOGUE

On the morning of 15 May 1922, more than 1,200 recruits of the newly established Civic Guard suddenly broke ranks during the commissioner's address at morning parade in the training depot at Kildare Barracks. The dissident recruits immediately set about raiding the armoury, while the commissioner and his senior officers withdrew under armed protection and evacuated the barracks, much to the annoyance of Michael Collins, the chairman of the fledgling Provisional Government. For almost seven weeks, Collins and the mutineers struggled to reconcile their differences in the midst of the Irish Civil War. This book investigates the reasons why these early recruits of the Civic Guard took up arms against their own masters, bringing about a significant security risk that had direct implications for both the Civil War and the future structure of the Civic Guard's successor, An Garda Síochána.

Michael Staines, Quartermaster-General, Irish Volunteers
(*c.* 1916). He was appointed commissioner of the Civic Guard in
1922. *Courtesy of the Garda Museum and Archives.*

INTRODUCTION

To date, the events surrounding the Civic Guard Mutiny of 1922 have remained one of Ireland's best-kept historical secrets. Despite the presence of relevant files in the National Archives of Ireland, the mutiny has largely been overlooked or hastily summarised in publications devoted to the history of Irish policing, regardless of the direct involvement of many senior Irish political figures. Indeed, the events of the mutiny have been neglected by historical commentators to such an extent that in the 1960s one veteran of the dispute wrote a series of short articles about the mutiny entitled 'Smothered History'.[1]

To appreciate the complexities of the mutiny, an understanding of the historical background of Irish policing is necessary. My primary focus here concerns the decision of the Provisional Government to establish a new police force modelled on the disbanded and world-renowned Royal Irish Constabulary (RIC), which had been the target of republican attacks in the War of Independence between 1919 and 1921. The transition of police power from the RIC to the Civic Guard is identified as the moment that the Provisional Government failed to take decisive action to avert an imminent mutiny. This book examines the actual events of the mutiny, but a significant part of it is also concerned with the repercussions for the force. The assessment of the aftermath of the mutiny is helped by the reports from the official enquiry into the dispute, which provided a series of recommendations for the future of Irish policing that have been preserved and embraced by An Garda Síochána. I would like to thank the National Archives of Ireland and the Director of the National Archives of Ireland for permission to reproduce parts of the commission of enquiry into the mutiny, as well as other relevant texts in their collection.

1

POLICING IN IRELAND BEFORE 1922

In 1169, on the orders of King Henry II, the successful Anglo-Norman invasion of Ireland took place. In 1204, King John of England commissioned the construction of a stone castle in Dublin to become the headquarters of the new administration in Ireland and the result, Dublin Castle, would remain the headquarters of British administrative and political control in the country until the establishment of the Irish Free State in 1922. It was at Dublin Castle that Michael Staines, the commissioner of Ireland's first national police force, the Civic Guard, was granted the symbolic privilege of leading a batch of the force's new recruits to relieve the remaining British personnel of their duties, an event which took place on 17 August 1922.[1] When approaching the history of policing in Ireland that led to this significant moment for the new Irish Free State, it is necessary to travel as far back as 1199.

In that year John, the youngest son of Henry II, acceded to the throne and ordered the gradual division of Ireland into counties. It was decreed that robbers 'be driven out of our land in Ireland, and that they and those who receive them be dealt with according to the law of England' (9 John, AD 1207).[2] The implementation of John's policies facilitated the systematic replacement of the native Irish system of Brehon Law with English laws and administration.

No overall authority had existed to administer or enforce Brehon Law, although trained judges mediated in disputes of a criminal or civil nature. The social standing of the offender determined the amount of compensation to be paid and it was normal for both parties to hire an advocate to present cases before a judge.[3] This absence of a law enforcement agency in Gaelic Ireland contrasted with the situation in England and was something John's successors would seek to remedy. In 1285 the terms of the Statute of Winchester obliged each county of Ireland to abandon Brehon Law and accept the authority of English justices of the peace to hear criminal and civil cases (1 Edward II, AD 1308).[4] The statute regulated a nightwatch system in towns and cities, supervised by two high constables. All resident males, including native Irishmen, between fifteen and sixty years of age were to take their turn as nightwatchmen at each town gate, although the Irish were prohibited from holding the positions of mayor, bailiff or any office of the king.

The provisions of the Statute of Winchester were amended continuously, and between the thirteenth and eighteenth centuries provided the basis for a policing system. For centuries, the successful transition to English Law within Ireland largely occurred in the towns and cities, while the Gaelic lords preserved their traditional customs and laws in the rest of the country. However, Henry VIII's policy of 'surrender and regrant', instituted in the 1540s, threatened Gaelic lords with confiscation of their lands unless they surrendered their titles and assumed alternative English titles, customs and laws. As a result, most Gaelic and Anglo-Irish subjects accepted the kingship of the English monarch and the attendant customs and laws, although they tended to repudiate the subsequent espousal of the Protestant faith, much to the annoyance of the English monarchy.

On her ascent to the throne, Elizabeth I continued her father's policy of extending crown control over Ireland. A rebellion led by the prominent lords of Munster in 1579 was crushed by the forces of the crown. Elizabeth confiscated their lands and transferred ownership to loyal Protestant colonists. Following the settlement of loyal English colonists in large areas of Munster, it was anticipated that the final displacement of native Irish Brehon laws and customs would be achieved effectively. Yet the celebrated poet and English planter in Munster, Edmund Spenser, contested the policy of forcing English Law on the native Irish population. In his capacity as secretary to Sir Arthur Grey, lord deputy of Ireland, Spenser argued that it was naïve to expect the English legal system to function in Ireland merely on the basis that it was already operating successfully in England:

> … for laws ought to be fashioned unto the manners and conditions of the people to whom they are meant, and not to be imposed upon them according to the simple rule of right, for then … instead of good they may work ill and pervert justice to extreme unjustice.[5]

In Ulster, the Gaelic lords feared a similar fate to that of their dispossessed counterparts in Munster and began to secure military support from Spain. The defeat of the Gaelic lords and Spaniards at the Battle of Kinsale in 1601 effectively ensured the end of the native Irish ruling class. The subsequent plantation of Ulster with Scottish and English Protestant immigrants followed the hasty departure of the Gaelic lords to the safety of the Continent.

In the wake of the Battle of Kinsale, the English authorities sought to weaken the numerical supremacy of the native Irish in Ireland and expedited the influx of loyal subjects who would abide by English Common Law. By 1641 there were 22,000 planters in Munster and 15,000 in the province of Ulster.[6] This policy was based on the premise that loyalty to the crown could be imported from England and Scotland: 'If the Irish would not become Protestant, then Protestants must be brought to Ireland.'[7]

On three occasions during the seventeenth century, Irish Catholic forces fought unsuccessfully against Protestant armies for supremacy in Ireland. The victory of William of Orange at the Battle of the Boyne in 1690 finally ensured the permanency of the planters and terminated decisively any lingering aspirations the native Irish had of securing ownership of lost lands. The last remaining and besieged Catholic force accepted the terms of the Treaty of Limerick in October 1691, and the supremacy of Protestants in Ireland was assured and safeguarded by their own Irish parliament. The enactment of a comprehensive series of anti-Catholic measures, the 'Penal

Laws', ensured that the Protestant ruling class would be in a position of ascendancy over the native Irish population. Catholics were excluded from the legal profession, parliament and government office, and banned from holding commissions in the army or navy. Such legislation effectively restricted the advancement of the native Irish in society. Furthermore, 'An Act to refrain papists from being high or petty constables and for the better regulating of the parish watches' (2 Geo. I, c. 10) was introduced in 1715.[8] From that point onwards, constables were required to take the following oath:

> I do solemnly and sincerely, in the presence of God, profess, testify and declare, that I do believe, that in the sacrament of the lord's supper there is not any transubstantiation of the elements of bread and wine into the body and blood of Christ, at or after the consecration thereof by any person whatsoever: and that the invocation, or adoration of the virgin Mary, or any other saint, and the sacrifice of the mass, as they are now used in the church of Rome, are superstitious and idolatrous.[9]

The enactment of further anti-Catholic legislation in 1704 and 1709 prohibited Catholics from buying land, inheriting land from Protestants and taking leases for more than thirty-one years. By 1778 Catholic ownership of land in the country had been reduced to five per cent from eighteen per cent in 1704, and the greater part of the Irish countryside gradually entered a system of domination by Protestant landlords, who were largely supported by Catholic tenant subsistence farming.[10] The maintenance of law and order in such a divided social setting was of paramount importance to the English authorities.

POLICE REFORM IN THE EIGHTEENTH CENTURY

The Irish political framework provided a parliament composed almost exclusively of Protestant members and drawn from a narrow franchise. However, supreme authority rested with the representative of the English crown in Ireland, the lord lieutenant, otherwise referred to as the 'viceroy'. The chief secretary assisted the lord lieutenant in the formulation of national policy and together they effectively ruled the country.[11] In 1715 grand juries were established in each of the 300 baronies in Ireland. All baronies were required to appoint a high constable to supervise the watch system, which by this time could employ only Protestants. The appointed watchmen were authorised to stop and search people, and on finding any who could not give a satisfactory account of their activities, were empowered to bring them before the local justice.[12] By the 1760s, the ineffectiveness of the baronial constables was illustrated by the degree of agrarian violence carried out by native Irish peasants, who formed a secret society of 'Whiteboys'. The organisation frustrated the constables by engaging in harmful acts against agents, animals and properties of landlords in County Tipperary and surrounding counties.[13]

The collective and localised violence of the Whiteboys was soon escalated by a new secret society, the Rightboys. In 1785 the Rightboys launched a campaign of violence against the payment of tithes to the Anglican church. The movement appealed to a wider social base than the Whiteboys, as the Right-boys also protested forcibly against levels of rents and taxes.

Unrest in Ireland attracted the attention of the British authorities, who had recently failed in their endeavour to introduce the London and Westminster Police Bill of 1785, which sought to establish a government-controlled, full-time professional police force for London.[14] Opponents of the bill claimed that the extensive powers of the proposed force were too radical and extreme.[15] Under mounting pressure from the press and public opinion, the British prime minister, William Pitt, withdrew the offending bill and promised to submit an alternative policing legislative measure in due course. The British government looked towards Ireland as the appropriate experimental venue for its proposed police force. The uncertain prevailing circumstances of agrarian violence, coupled with civil unrest in towns and cities as various classes demanded concessions from the British government in the wake of revolutions in America and France, prompted the Irish authorities reluctantly to accept the directives from the English government to enact two substantial police bills.

The Dublin Police Act of 1786 (26 Geo. III, c. 24) was the first decree of British legislation to include the French word 'police', used in terms of 'keeping order'.[16] This act also established the first modern police force in the United Kingdom, and allowed for experimentation in policing before similar strategies were embarked on in England, Scotland and Wales. Commentators have continued to cite the Dublin Police Act of 1786 as the forerunner to the establishment of modern police forces throughout Britain: '[A] full history of the new police would probably lay its first scene in Ireland and begin with the Dublin Police Act passed by the Irish Parliament in 1786.'[17] This was the first occasion that Ireland was used as a 'social laboratory' for experiments the English government was not prepared to contemplate in England.[18] Subsequent use of Ireland as a convenient venue for experimentation occurred between 1786 and 1838, in areas such as welfare, planning and education.[19]

The *Dublin Evening Post* of March 1786 openly condemned the bill and accused Pitt's administration of succumbing to English public opinion over the contentious issue of police reform and smuggling the spurned bill into an undiscerning Ireland.[20] Thomas Orde, the Irish chief secretary at the time, was given responsibility for the replacement of the traditional nightwatch model of law enforcement with the first centralised force of policemen in the United Kingdom. For policing purposes, Dublin, with a population of 150,000, was divided into four districts and placed under the authority of Dublin Castle. The commissioners were obliged to recruit men who were young and in good health. Though the population of Dublin was approximately seventy-five per cent Catholic in composition, only Protestants were entitled to seek employment in a force consisting of 400 men.[21] Successful applicants were to be dressed in the prescribed blue uniforms and bear arms consisting of bayonets and muskets.[22]

In 1787 the English government, satisfied with the initial progress of the police innovation in Dublin, introduced similar legislation to the rest of the country through 'The Irish

County Act', the immediate implementation of which sought to suppress the campaign of the Rightboys in their stronghold counties of Tipperary, Kerry, Kilkenny and Cork. Under the terms of the act, each of the 300 baronies in Ireland was to be provided with a chief constable and sixteen sub-constables. A provision excluding Catholics from employment within the force was included in the act.

Despite Grattan subsequently introducing legislation to modify policing arrangements in Dublin, the United Irishmen Rebellion of 1798 immediately transformed the Irish political scene and had a major impact on security arrangements for the country. The Catholic and Protestant insurgents of the United Irishmen had obtained French assistance in their quest for Irish independence from England, but nevertheless were routed. Despite their failure, with a death toll of 30,000 the rebellion reawakened fears that the Irish parliament was not capable of containing political agitation without strong reliance on support from England. In the aftermath of the rebellion, the Irish parliament approved a more centralised form of policing, as contained in the Dublin Police Act of 1799, and agreed to terminate its own existence by approving the Act of Union in 1800, which reintroduced direct rule from the English parliament at Westminster and 'sought to bind Ireland more closely to Britain through a policy of cultural assimilation'.[23] In actuality, the responsibility for day-to-day Irish affairs was still entrusted to the authorities in Dublin Castle, under the direction of the lord lieutenant and the chief secretary, and it was at this juncture that the more fervent nationalists started to identify the police as the 'eyes and ears' of Dublin Castle.[24]

THE 'PEELERS'

In September 1812 Robert Peel, at the age of twenty-four, was appointed chief secretary of Ireland. Peel soon identified agrarian protest movements and the possibility of another rebellion as the most threatening issues confronting the authorities at Dublin Castle. In June 1814 Peel established a mobile force of uniformed and armed policemen controlled by Dublin Castle and officially referred to as the Peace Preservation Force (PPF). Significantly, the PPF (or 'Peelers' as they were popularly known) became the first police force in the United Kingdom to recruit Catholics, who accounted for 16 per cent of the 2,326 men enlisted until the force was allowed to dissolve on a gradual basis between 1822 and 1828.[25]

In 1822 Peel was appointed home secretary and continued his reform of policing in Ireland with the establishment of the County Constabulary, which was to be a permanent armed police force under the control of Dublin Castle. The 313 chief constables were to conduct monthly inspections and ensure that the 5,000 constables adhered to the regulations. The vast majority of the constables were the sons of farmers, while the higher-ranking members were drawn from the ascendancy classes.[26] The County Constabulary was the first Irish police force to require its members to undergo three months of training conducted by military instructors at four provincial training centres. The code of the force expressed the need for constables 'never to use more force, or violence than is absolutely necessary' and, as public servants to the crown, a degree of impartiality towards the public was to be observed.[27]

The exacting standards demanded by police barrack regulations were in contrast to the abject poverty and living conditions associated with the lower classes of Irish society. Members of the County Constabulary were to provide an example of morality to the impoverished masses.[28] Though the force was largely Protestant in composition, its deployment in the countryside was aided by its policy of recruiting a greater number of Catholics than had been the case under the PPF. It is significant that during this period the leader of the Catholic Association, Daniel O'Connell, recommended that Catholics should seize the opportunity of a career in the County Constabulary as it would provide much-needed employment, end discrimination and thereby support the campaign for Catholic emancipation.

While policing in Ireland was slowly becoming more representative, it simultaneously assumed a distinctly military appearance through the provision of barracks throughout the country. Each policeman was heavily armed with a sabre, pistol, short carbine with attached bayonet, and sixty rounds of ball cartridge.[29] By the 1820s the strength of the County Constabulary was edging towards 6,000, and the chief secretary, Henry Goulburn, advised Peel that a smaller military presence in Ireland was expected as a result of the pressures of foreign military campaigns, so it was necessary for the County Constabulary uniquely to combine the duties of a police and military force to maintain law and order in Ireland. Though the loyalty and efficiency of the County Constabulary was not tested by the mass campaign for Catholic emancipation, which was resolved peacefully in April 1829, the divisive issues of tithes and of O'Connell's crusade to repeal the Act of Union placed the police in a precarious position. Between 1830 and 1832, an escalation of rioting occurred among tenants. The prevalence of agrarian unrest necessitated the reintroduction of the PPF to assist the County Constabulary in the collection of tithes. Forty-four tenants and twenty-three County Constables died in disturbances during the Tithe War (1830–6).[30] Despite the Catholic composition of the County Constabulary, the force was increasingly perceived as the enforcer of English and Protestant rule in Ireland. The County Constabulary responded to tenant hostility by withdrawing from its thatched barracks and moving into better-fortified accommodation.

Drummond's Two Police Forces

In the 1830s Dublin Castle confronted the threat of ongoing agrarian unrest through the centralisation of Irish policing. Two separate police forces were established: the Irish Constabulary and the Dublin Metropolitan Police (DMP). The Irish under-secretary, Thomas Drummond, drafted the legislation for the creation of both forces – the Police Reform Act of 1836.

The Irish Constabulary was a semi-military police force with responsibility for policing most of the country. Drummond intensified his efforts to seek greater public acceptance for the new force by recruiting a higher proportion of Catholics. Though the senior ranks of the force were reserved for former British army officers, Catholics accounted for two-thirds of the lower ranks of the new force.[31] Furthermore, Drummond modified the traditional policy of recruiting the sons of farmers to include the labouring class, especially from the north-westerly counties of Roscommon, Leitrim, Sligo, Cavan and Fermanagh.[32] The radical overhaul of the Irish national school system in 1831 by the chief secretary, Edward G. Stanley, ensured that the Irish Constabulary would be provided with a steady supply of suitably qualified men eager for recruitment to the lower ranks of the force. The basic entrance requirements to the force demanded that candidates be aged between nineteen and twenty-seven years, at least 5ft 8in (1.7 metres) in height and 'capable of reading, without hesitation, any printed or written document and able to write legible hand'.[33] The considerable expansion of the national school system effectively provided a basic education for all children in Ireland, regardless of creed. By 1860 there were seven times more national schools in the country than there had been in 1833.[34]

Year	Number of schools	Number of pupils[35]
1833	789	107,042
1840	1,978	232,560
1850	4,547	511,239
1860	5,632	804,000

In addition, each candidate was required to be single and display honesty, sobriety and fidelity. A three-month training programme was undertaken at the purpose-built training depot in Phoenix Park, Dublin, which was opened in 1842.

By 1843 the Irish Constabulary had established more than 1,400 barracks throughout the country. The strategic positioning of these ensured that during occasions of public disorder or rebellion in any area of the country there was a barracks that could be called upon.[36] In his book, *Ireland*, the German travel writer, Johann Georg Kohl, describes his impression of the force in the first few months of its existence:

> The police station, which lay on our road, and at which we stopped, was a new, neat, spacious building. At a short distance it appeared like a little strong castle. The house contained eight men of the constabulary force, as it is called, and which is a military-armed police, now extended over the whole of Ireland, for the prevention of crime, the discovery and apprehension of criminals, the protection of property, and the preservation of the peace. It consists of 8,000 men, classified and disciplined in the same manner as soldiers … They are armed with carbines and swords, and also use their bayonets as daggers. They differ from the soldiers in their uniform alone, which is somewhat less ornamented and a dark green colour. This police force is, therefore, properly a military garrison, though under another name. Since the strongest men, and those only of the most unblemished characters, are admitted into this force, and then distributed into every corner of the land, they possess an extremely intimate knowledge of it and of its inhabitants, and in

the event of a war or a rebellion would probably be more valuable than an army of 30,000 men.[37]

In the early years of the force, its inspector-general, James Shaw-Kennedy, issued a comprehensive code of regulations for the Irish Constabulary, much of which was drawn upon by subsequent Irish police forces up to the mid-twentieth century.[38] The code specifically outlined the duties and regulations for the maintenance of a disciplined force to the extent that the Irish Constabulary maintained the 'toughest and most uncompromising code of regulations of any police force in the world'.[39] The appointment of ex-military personnel to high-ranking positions within the force ensured a heavy emphasis on efficiency and discipline. In terms of their relationship with the local upper classes, the constabulary's performance of the duties of gamekeeping and private protection ceased. However, members of the lower and middle ranks were required to be respected by the people and 'obtain the good opinion of the gentry'.[40] In addition to the local priest, members of the Irish Constabulary were often the only source of literacy in the locality. The Irish Constabulary drew on such public reliance for the gathering of intelligence and obliged its members to fortify their position through additional duties to the extent that 'everything in Ireland, from the muzzling of a dog to the suppression of a rebellion is done by the Irish Constabulary'.[41] To this end, the police evolved into an agency of local government and assumed responsibility for road regulations, census taking, weights and measures inspections, and the collection of agricultural statistics.[42]

In contrast to the military appearance of the Irish Constabulary, the DMP consisted of 900 unarmed men. By the 1840s the members of that force were involved in the detection of crime and vice in Dublin city, where the population had increased to more than 200,000.[43] Despite sharing similar training regimes, entrance criteria and composition of personnel, the fortunes of the DMP and the Irish Constabulary would contrast sharply in succeeding decades because of political upheaval. In contrast to the armed members of the Irish Constabulary, the constables of the DMP enjoyed wider public acceptance, and they were not the target of agrarian and political unrest.

POLICING POLITICAL UPHEAVAL

Within a decade of the establishment of the Irish Constabulary and the DMP, the country was in the grip of the Great Famine, following successive outbreaks of potato blight in the mid-1840s. High rates of mortality and emigration reduced the Irish population of eight million by one-fifth between 1845 and 1851.[44] Fearing bankruptcy, many landlords further compounded the misery of impecunious tenants by evicting those who were in rent arrears.[45] In 1849 the Irish Constabulary recorded 90,000 evictions; a year later the number was in excess of 100,000.[46] The involvement of the Irish Constabulary in the processes of eviction reinforced the claim by its critics that the police were mere agents of the landlords and British rule.

Following the death of Daniel O'Connell in 1847, a void was left in Irish politics, which extreme nationalism sought to fill by organising itself into an oath-bound secret society, the Irish Republican Brotherhood (IRB), in 1858. The estimated 60,000 members of the IRB were referred to as Fenians and, under the leadership of James Stephens, a rebellion was planned. The Irish Constabulary succeeded in monitoring the movements of the society and thwarted their attempts to obtain and distribute arms among their members. On 5 March 1867, the Fenians rebelled and attacked many Irish Constabulary barracks, almost exclusively in the southern half of Ireland. The effective military training of the well-armed Irish Constabulary ensured limited and only momentary success for the insurgents at three barracks. Following the arrest of 169 men, both the House of Commons and the House of Lords in London applauded the Irish Constabulary, and nine members of the force were decorated for valour.[47] In recognition of their successful suppression of the Rising, Queen Victoria bestowed the title 'Royal Irish Constabulary' (RIC) on the force on 6 September 1867. Nationalist critics regarded the conferment of the title 'Royal' on the force as a reward for the Irish Constabulary's unwavering loyalty to the British crown and its determination to preserve the political and social status quo. In the aftermath of the Fenian Rising, Lord Derby addressed the House of Lords and proclaimed his surprise that a police force which was largely composed of ordinary Irishmen could demonstrate such commitment in suppressing unrest among their own people:

This body of police are sprung from that class of the people, amongst whom, if amongst any, there are likely to be found the seeds of discontent; and yet, in no case was there the slightest disloyalty amongst them; and their determined and successful efforts to suppress this insurrection have been nothing short of actual heroism.[48]

In 1877 Michael Davitt was released from Dartmoor prison after serving seven years for his part in the trafficking of arms for the IRB in London. On witnessing the high levels of poverty and eviction in his native area of County Mayo in 1879, Davitt organised a public meeting of 15,000 people in Irishtown, which led to the establishment of the Irish National Land League in October of that year. Davitt claimed that the RIC were the upholders of an Irish landlord system that was based on the exploitation of tenant farmers and labourers. He asserted that an Irishman can 'have no feeling of respect towards the RIC, because he knows that it is an Imperial political force, having none of the qualities of a police body, and that its extra-political *raison d'être* is to form a bodyguard for the system of Irish landlordism'.[49]

Among the primary objectives of the league were the prevention of unjust evictions and the attainment of land ownership by tenant farmers. The presidency of the league was bestowed on Charles Stewart Parnell, MP, leader of the largest political organisation in Ireland, the Irish Parliamentary Party, at the inaugural meeting on 21 October. During his leadership, from 1879 to 1882, a period of intense agrarian unrest referred to as the 'Land War' unfolded. The league provided support and shelter to evicted families, and people deemed to have violated the code of the Land League were socially ostracised or 'boycotted'.[50] Despite the non-violent methods of the Land League, the more extreme supporters were responsible for an explosion of serious agrarian crime. In 1879, 863 cases of agrarian crime had been reported, but by 1881 the annual number of cases had increased five-fold.[51] The decision by the British government to increase the supply of ammunition to the force and to require that RIC members assist bailiffs and landlords in evicting tenants, only served to reinforce the notion that the police were upholding the landlord system.

The hardship endured by the RIC in dealing with the more violent events of the 'Land War' was relieved temporarily in March 1882, following successful negotiations between Prime Minister William Gladstone and Parnell, who had been arrested for sedition and was being held in Kilmainham Jail. The introduction of state-aided land-purchase schemes effectively curtailed the power of Irish landlords, as large numbers of Irish tenant farmers were helped by the British government to purchase their own land. Parnell's success in agrarian matters allowed him to concentrate on the attainment of Irish Home Rule. However, the public revelation in 1889 of his adultery with Mrs Katherine O'Shea divided the Irish Parliamentary Party and rendered it an ineffective force in Irish politics for the following decade.

THE DEMISE OF THE RIC

The public perception of the RIC became more agreeable in the wake of Parnell's death, as the force was no longer confronted with an organised nationalist political movement. However, as the nineteenth century drew to a close, the emergence of non-political movements began to overshadow the effectiveness of the divided Irish Parliamentary Party, and gradually a wave of resentment towards the RIC began to resurface. In 1884 the Gaelic Athletic Association (GAA) was established, and the provision of codified rules for the playing of native Irish games provided the basis for the rapid expansion of the movement. The organisation was outspokenly nationalist and attracted many IRB members. Significantly, the GAA enacted rules that forbade its members from playing or even watching 'imported games', and excluded RIC and DMP personnel from registering as members. This exclusion of Irish police members was based primarily on the suspicion that they were 'the principal source of information on the strength and disposition of all nationalist activity'.[52]

Meanwhile, the Anglo-Irish literary revival, led by William Butler Yeats, romanticised ancient Irish legendary heroes and portrayed Ireland as an old woman who could be restored as queen only through the heroic actions of her countrymen. In addition to the sporting and literary revivals, the Gaelic League, established by Douglas Hyde and Eoin MacNeill in 1893, sought to restore the Irish language as the spoken tongue of the country. However, Hyde earnestly attempted to prevent the Gaelic League from being permeated by IRB members and resigned in protest when the leadership of the organisation finally succumbed to the influence of nationalist extremists.

Ironically, as the silent outbreak of cultural nationalism spread throughout Ireland in the early twentieth century, the RIC enjoyed a period of relative calm. In 1900 the three-week royal visit by Queen Victoria and her family to Ireland was widely welcomed by the Irish people and the security arrangements of the RIC and DMP earned each member a medal to commemorate the historic event. The successful royal visit emphasised the notion that policing in Ireland was enjoying a period of civil tranquillity. From 1900, with the widespread availability of the bicycle, sections of the police code were relaxed. Consequently, off-duty RIC members were no longer required to remain in the barracks, and only those who were finishing duty were detailed to attend the nightly roll call at 11 p.m.[53] Indeed, the RIC received favourable editorial comments even in the nationalist pamphlet, *United Irishman*, where Arthur Griffith, co-founder of the Sinn Féin political party, wrote:

The Royal Irish Constabulary is a body of Irishmen, recruited from the Irish people. They are bone of their bone, and flesh of their flesh. The typical young constabulary man is Irish and of the Irish, Catholic and (as the word goes) Nationalist; the son of decent parents; his father a Home Rule farmer; his uncle a patriotic priest; his cousin a nun; his sweetheart the daughter of a local Nationalist District Councillor and patriotic publican;

her uncle being chairman of the local 'league' branch and a friend of the eloquent and patriotic member for the Division, who asks questions on the floor about the young constabulary man's prospects and grievances. The young constabulary man subscribes liberally to the Church; he is smiled on by the Irish clergy; he is smiled on by the Irish girls; he is respected by the young fellows of the street corner and the country crossroads.[54]

By 1900 the RIC was arguably perceived as being 'the best police force in the world'.[55] The training regime endured by recruits at the renowned Phoenix Park Depot ensured a high level of military efficiency, combined with a thorough knowledge of police duties and procedures. Colonel Neville Chamberlain succeeded Andrew Reed in 1900 as the inspector general of the RIC. During his sixteen-year tenure, Chamberlain demanded a higher degree of civility from his force and issued instructions to all personnel regarding the maintenance of exemplary standards of public courtesy. Failure to comply with the directive would seriously impede the promotional prospects of even the most qualified and educated members of the force:

Every policeman who desires advancement in the Royal Irish Constabulary should make courtesy and politeness to the general public his special study. These qualities are as important for study and improvement as the subjects of drill and police duties. Officers of the Force are directed (and in the interests of the Service they should ever bear in mind) to recommend no man for promotion who is arrogant, rude, rough, or unmannerly in dealing with the public; and this direction should be acted on whether such a man has been successful in the detection of crime, possesses superior education and can pass examinations with success.[56]

The internationally high regard enjoyed by the RIC attracted many tours of inspection of the training regime in the early years of the twentieth century. The force's elevated standing was assured by its continuous supply of suitable personnel for service to the colonial police forces of the British Empire. As the only British armed police force exposed to deep-rooted political turmoil, the RIC demonstrated a high degree of proficiency in overcoming the difficulties of policing a relatively hostile colony. The Colonial Office in London became particularly reliant on obtaining the services of high-ranking RIC members for positions in the various colonies. Consequently, many of the colonial and territorial forces, including the North West Mounted Police in Canada, the Auckland Armed Police Force in New Zealand and the Indian Police, were established mainly using the RIC model.[57] The exceptional training standards maintained by the RIC motivated the Colonial Office in London to instigate an investigation into the training procedures at the Phoenix Park Depot. In May 1905 the under secretary of state, Colonial Office, Roland V. Vernon, furnished the secretary of state, Colonial Office, with a glowing report on the RIC in terms of its organisation and methods of selecting officers, and Vernon requested that the Colonial Office oblige the RIC to assume responsibility for training all newly appointed colonial officers for a period of approximately six months: 'The Royal Irish Constabulary is the only institution in the United Kingdom which has the means of giving proper instruction to officers of a semi-military police force ... and the Imperial Government ought not to grudge the Colonies assistance in supplying that training in the only institution competent to give it.'[58]

In 1907 the Colonial Office acceded to Vernon's request. From that time, the training of all colonial police officers of commissioned rank was to be conducted at the RIC training depot at Phoenix Park. Within four years, more than 100 exclusively white and British-born commissioned officers received their training from RIC instructors. In 1912 RIC police instructor Robert Sparrow submitted an article to the *RIC Magazine* about the training of colonial officers in Dublin, and posed the rhetorical question as to why the RIC rather than another British police force had been requested to conduct the training programme. He continued:

The answer is simple. No British police force is officered by cadets or armed with rifle and bayonet except the Royal Irish Constabulary, and the Colonial police are officered, armed and drilled and trained more after the fashion and on the lines of the Irish than of any other British police force, and their officers would naturally be sent for training to the alma mater of that Force on which they themselves are modelled. They have, at the Depot in the Phoenix Park, all the facilities for learning everything connected with their future profession, except of course, local colouring, custom and language, the knowledge of which must be acquired on the spot.[59]

Despite the international acclaim enjoyed by the RIC in the early years of the twentieth century, the force at a domestic level suffered a gradual alienation in the face of the emerging power of Irish nationalism, which increasingly questioned the ethos of the force. While the original intention of the Gaelic League and the GAA had been to nurture Irish national identity through the promotion of the Irish language and native games, their infiltration by the IRB intensified the drive for self-determination and political separation from Britain. Patrick Pearse, a member of the Supreme Council of the IRB, recognised at an early stage the political influence that the Irish language movement would have on Irish independence: 'The Gaelic League will be recognised in history as the most revolutionary influence that has ever come to Ireland. The Irish revolution really began when the seven proto-Gaelic Leaguers met in O'Connell Street … The germ of all future Irish history was in that back room.'[60]

The support for fervent nationalism was curtailed temporarily but effectively by the success of John Redmond's Irish Parliamentary Party in the British general election of 1910. The failure of the Liberal Party to retain an overall majority in the election provided Redmond with the opportunity to offer parliamentary support to the weakened government in return for the resurrection of the Home Rule issue. In 1912 the Irish Party was rewarded with the passing of a Home Rule bill in the House of Commons. However, the House of Lords rejected the proposed legislation and enactment of the bill was postponed for two years.

The new leader of the Irish Unionist Party, Edward Carson, set about organising opposition to what unionists considered the offensive proposal of Home Rule. Carson and his supporters argued that the planned devolved Irish parliament would facilitate economic, social and religious discrimination against the minority unionist contingent. By early 1913, 100,000 men in the unionist stronghold of north-east Ulster had enlisted as members of the Ulster Volunteer Force (UVF), an armed resistance movement formed to oppose the expected enactment of the third Home Rule Act in 1914, with armed force if necessary. With no RIC or military interference, the UVF successfully smuggled from Germany 24,600 rifles and three million rounds of ammunition into the Ulster ports of Larne, Donaghadee and Bangor.[61] The impotent response of the forces of law and order was a significant factor that encouraged nationalists to establish a similar armed volunteer force in November 1913 for the defence of the Home Rule legislation. Under John Redmond, the Irish Volunteers successfully recruited 160,000 men.

The issue of Home Rule was shelved by its suspension at the start of the First World War in 1914. The UVF and the National Volunteers, who had split from the Irish Volunteers over the issue of supporting the British in the war effort, sent large numbers of men to fight in the British regiments. However, the remaining Irish Volunteers, who were vehemently opposed to the provision of Irishmen for the British army, instead secretly planned a rising across the country. The successful RIC interception at Banna Beach, County Kerry, of German rifles and machine guns destined for the rebels, led Eoin MacNeill, leader of the Volunteer movement, to cancel the planned action. However, a small section of the Dublin-based Volunteers disobeyed MacNeill and led a Rising in the city centre of Dublin on Easter Monday, 24 April 1916.

After a week of fighting, the rebels surrendered to the British military, and following the executions of the rebel leaders, a shift in public opinion against the British occurred. In response to a plea from the deputy leader of the Irish Party, John Dillon, to spare the lives of the leaders, the supreme commanding officer of the British army in Ireland, General Sir John Maxwell, replied, 'I am going to punish the offenders, four of them are to be shot tomorrow morning. I am going to ensure that there will be no treason whispered, even whispered, in Ireland for a hundred years.'[62]

Notwithstanding their lack of involvement during the week's activities, the RIC had to endure the release of public wrath as an unexpected swing of support towards republicanism unfolded. In the recollections of one RIC man, 'The change in the attitude of the people of the district towards British rule in Ireland between Easter 1916 and June 1918 was astonishing. It was a continual and gradual process and at the beginning was hardly perceptible.'[63] The slow manifestation of public resentment towards the police was identified by the county inspector of Clare, who officially noted in September 1916 that the recent police recruiting programme had uncharacteristically brought little response and that the people of the county were generally less friendly towards the force. A year later, the county inspector recorded, 'The people appear to regard the police as their enemies, and have ceased all friendly intercourse with them. Shops continue to supply provisions but in many cases they would prefer the police did not come to them.'[64]

As Irish public opinion became increasingly hostile during the executions of the rebels, the British authorities decided to stop the killings after fifteen of the ninety main insurgents had been executed. The sentences of the remaining seventy-five rebels were commuted to penal servitude for life. The Sinn Féin political party, 'still a mere fringe nationalist faction' under the leadership of Arthur Griffith, was wrongly held responsible for the Easter Rising of 1916.[65] In the face of growing support for the Rising, however, the IRB soon infiltrated the party and it was quickly publicly perceived as the political wing of the militant republican movement. By October 1917 the extent of IRB influence over Sinn Féin was illustrated by the decision of Arthur Griffith to give up his position as president of the party to facilitate the appointment of his successor, Éamon de Valera, the senior surviving commandant of the Easter Rising.[66]

THE RIC AND THE WAR OF INDEPENDENCE

During 1917 a series of by-election results signified a decisive shift in public opinion, as Sinn Féin enjoyed increasing electoral success. The general election of December 1918 confirmed republicanism as the new power in Irish politics, with Sinn Féin securing seventy-three seats, the Unionists winning twenty-six and the Irish Party reduced to a mere six. In compliance with their election commitment, Sinn Féin refused to take their seats in Westminster. Instead, Sinn Féin TDs established their own parliament, Dáil Éireann, at the Mansion House in Dublin on 21 January 1919.[67] Despite an invitation to attend the inaugural session being issued to all elected Irish members of parliament, only twenty-seven Sinn Féin TDs were able to attend, because thirty-four of their representatives were in prison or on the run.[68] During the course of the inaugural session, Sinn Féin TDs demanded the immediate withdrawal of British military forces. On the same day, two RIC men, Constables James McDonnell and Patrick O'Connell, were ambushed and shot dead at Soloheadbeg in County Tipperary. Escorting a cartload of gelignite, they were set upon by local members of the Irish Volunteers.[69] The deaths at Soloheadbeg are generally accepted as the start of the War of Independence, and following the outbreak of this conflict the Volunteers became more commonly known by the name of Irish Republican Army (IRA). In his recollections of the killings, the commanding officer of the local republicans, Dan Breen, showed little remorse: 'Our only regret was that the police escort had consisted of only two peelers instead of six. If there had to be dead peelers at all, six would have created a better impression than a mere two.'[70]

Despite the initial public outrage, the direct involvement of the RIC during the two and a half years of the War of Independence eventually eroded any remaining sympathy or support for the police among moderate nationalist supporters. It is estimated that the final casualties amounted to 624 police and British military, and 752 IRA members and civilians.[71] Within two days of the ambush at Soloheadbeg, Dr Fogarty, Bishop of Killaloe, controversially justified military action against the police by stating that the fight for Irish freedom had passed into the hands of the young men of Ireland and that it was not the place for a man of his age to condemn such violence.[72] In the official magazine of the IRA, *An t-Óglach* (*The Volunteer*), General Headquarters (GHQ) supported the actions of Breen and his men at Soloheadbeg and declared that all IRA personnel were entitled both legally and morally 'to use all legitimate methods of warfare against the soldiers and policemen of the English usurper, and to slay them if necessary to do so to overcome their resistance'.[73]

Attacks on policemen were at first opposed but subsequently supported by de Valera. During a Dáil Éireann session on 9 April 1919, de Valera moved a resolution which declared that 'members of the police force acting in this country as part of the British occupation and as agents of the British be ostracised publicly and socially by the people of Ireland'.[74] To justify such a hostile act, de Valera maintained that the RIC was a force overtly intent on continuing British occupation in Ireland against the wishes of its people: 'The more brutal the commands given them by their superiors, the more they seem to revel in carrying them out, against their own flesh and blood, be it remembered. Their history is a continuity of brutal treason against their own people.'[75] The Irish public was instructed by Dáil Éireann to ostracise the RIC socially by not saluting policemen or allowing them to enter their private dwellings as friends or guests.[76] The twelve-year-old son of an RIC man stationed in Athlone, County Westmeath, Patrick Shea, recalled members of his family enduring physical and verbal intimidation. In addition to being labelled 'traitor' and 'English spy', Shea and his young brothers were reliant on his teacher to accompany them on their journey from school in the wake of a spate of attacks by some classmates.[77] The morale of the force was lowered severely by public ostracism, intimidation and IRA attacks on barracks. As the number of resignations mounted, potential recruits generally heeded IRA threats that a career in the police would have fatal consequences.

As attacks on RIC barracks continued during 1919, the force responded by withholding their civil dimension and instead assumed a militaristic appearance. Police stations were quickly transformed from being homely, whitewashed buildings into sandbagged, reinforced and heavily armed forts.[78] The redeployment of police to counties of strong IRA activity provoked many members into seeking alternative employment. By 1920 the monthly rate of RIC resignations had reached an average of 200 and a state of anarchy began to unfold in some areas of the countryside.[79]

Between 1919 and 1921, the IRA employed guerrilla warfare tactics against RIC and British military personnel. During this period, the Dáil Éireann minister for finance, Michael Collins, who held the position of director of IRA activities, emerged as a significant figure in the intelligence war. Collins carefully selected men to carry out special duties on his behalf. These men were referred to as 'the Squad' and were responsible for the fatal shootings of alleged spies or any personnel whom Collins perceived as being a threat to IRA operations. Collins successfully selected RIC and DMP personnel who were prepared to betray their British employers by furnishing him with the intelligence that allowed him to identify his enemies and elude capture.

The response of the British government to resignations from the force sealed the fate of the RIC. In March 1920 approximately 1,500 men from England, Scotland and Wales were assigned to the ranks of the waning RIC. The majority of the new recruits were former British soldiers who had served in the Great War. Because of a temporary shortage of RIC uniforms, they were obliged to wear a mixture of RIC and khaki attire, and such unorthodox police apparel earned the new recruits the title of 'Black and Tans'. They underwent a six-week intensive training regime, but unlike the RIC, the Black and Tans exacted revenge on the civilian population for attacks on them.

The mounting degree of hostility experienced by the RIC was not alleviated by the appointment in June 1920 of General H. H. Tudor to the position of chief of police in Ireland. On inspecting various RIC barracks, Tudor reported to the British government that his men were being boycotted and forced to live behind sandbags and wire entanglements.[80] Tudor, lacking in police experience, employed a military response by rearming the force with rifles and Lewis guns, and providing army-style Lancia and Crossley vehicles.[81] Within a few weeks of his appointment, Tudor established the Auxiliary division of the RIC, composed of elite demobilised officers of the British army. While the 'Auxies' were supposed to be under RIC command, the heavily armed 1,900 men generally operated independently of the police. Seven months after the establishment of the Auxiliaries, its commanding officer, Brigadier General Frank Percy Crozier, resigned in protest at the reinstatement of men under his command who had previously been charged with looting while on duty.

An incident at the RIC barracks in Listowel, County Kerry, in June 1920, provided IRA propagandists with a unique opportunity to portray the RIC as an oppressive force being used against the Irish people. Fourteen constables in Listowel refused to hand over their barracks to British soldiers as they feared the police in the area would be subjected to further public resentment on the eventual cessation of hostilities in the War of Independence. Rather than alleviating the anxieties of the constables, the RIC divisional commander in Munster, Colonel Smyth, attempted to bolster the morale of the men by encouraging them to exact lawless revenge on their enemies:

Now, men, Sinn Féin has had all the sport up to the present, and we are going to have sport now ... you may make mistakes occasionally, and innocent persons may be shot, but that cannot be helped, and you are bound to get the right parties sometime. The more you shoot, the better I will like you, and I assure you, no policeman will get into trouble for shooting any man.[82]

In response to Smyth's address, five RIC men left the force. All fourteen members of the RIC who had been present signed a transcript of the offensive address which was given to the local priest to dispatch to IRA headquarters for propaganda purposes.

While the RIC endured the worst of the IRA guerrilla activities, members of the DMP in June 1920 were ordered to bear arms and assist the British military in raids on suspected Sinn Féin offices. On experiencing fatal consequences in the wake of such developments, a delegation of the DMP met with IRA officers. It was agreed that the constables in Dublin city would refuse to carry arms and the IRA would cease to engage in hostile actions against the unarmed members.[83]

The IRA targeting of RIC personnel effectively curtailed the mobility of the police and forced closures of police stations across large areas of the countryside. As incidents of bank raids, land-grabbing and poitín distillation escalated, Dáil Éireann attempted to assert its claim to self-determination by providing an alternative system of law and order through the establishment of courts at the local level and the recruitment of a police force from the ranks of the IRA. While the Dáil Courts enjoyed a large degree of acceptance in most counties, the unarmed Irish Republican Police (IRP) 'proved ineffective and the quality of recruit to this force was a huge problem'.[84] IRA brigade officers were unwilling to assign their members during the War of Independence to such routine duties as 'chasing petty criminals and moonshiners'.[85] However, within specific areas of Munster, the IRP did achieve public support, which was recorded by a Downing Street correspondent in his report to the British government on 1 July 1920:

> I have just returned from a visit to my home in County Limerick. I found everything quite quiet. Sinn Féin rules the County – and rules it admirably. At our local races the Sinn Féin police controlled the traffic, the crowds, etc., 'parked' the motor cars, and in fact did all the work which has usually been done by the police, and did it excellently.[86]

During the course of the War of Independence, Lloyd George set up a committee to prepare for the establishment of Irish Home Rule. The main difficulty facing the committee involved the appeasement of contrasting unionist and nationalist aspirations. The primary recommendation of the committee involved the partition of Ireland into the two states of Northern Ireland and Southern Ireland. On 23 December 1920, the partition of Ireland, as accepted by the unionist leaders, was passed by parliament and came into effect on 3 May 1921.

A truce in July 1921 brought the War of Independence to a conclusion. In his capacity as minister for finance and adjutant of the IRA, Michael Collins agreed with Ireland's chief secretary, Sir Hamar Greenwood, that, for the duration of the Truce, the IRP and RIC would co-exist and co-operate through a liaison system.[87] Under such an arrangement, Dáil Éireann selected Michael Staines and Eoin O'Duffy as liaison officers, and both were involved subsequently in the establishment of a replacement force for the RIC.

2

THE REPLACEMENT OF THE RIC

Throughout the War of Independence, Sinn Féin publicly denounced RIC members as agents of crown control in Ireland. Though the ranks of the RIC were unquestionably awash with members sympathetic to the nationalist campaign, the ethos of the force was in stark contrast to popular aspirations. The establishment of a replacement force for the RIC in the new Irish political horizon was a primary concern for Michael Collins. While the inevitability of the disbandment of the RIC was assured, Collins and Hamar Greenwood agreed that the DMP could continue under any new political arrangement, as its unarmed members had maintained the respect and confidence of the general public.

During the course of the Truce, the president of Sinn Féin, Éamon de Valera, and the British prime minister, David Lloyd George, agreed to conclude their preliminary negotiations at a conference 'to ascertain how the association of Ireland with the community of nations known as the British Empire might best be reconciled with Irish national aspirations'.[1] Controversially, de Valera decided not to attend the London negotiations. Instead, Vice-President Arthur Griffith and

Michael Collins led the delegation to London on 11 October 1921. After almost two months of intense negotiations, both delegations signed the Anglo-Irish Treaty on 6 December. The partition of Ireland, which had already been enacted by the Government of Ireland Act 1920, was accepted by the Irish delegation. The states of Northern Ireland and the Irish Free State were to be self-governing dominions within the British Commonwealth.

However, de Valera and a sizeable minority of Dáil Éireann were unwilling to endorse an agreement that included constitutional links with Britain. In particular, the obligation on all Irish deputies to take an oath of allegiance to the monarch of England proved offensive to the republican principles of this faction.[2] On 7 January 1922, the Treaty was placed before Dáil Éireann for ratification and accepted by 64 votes to 57. The Sinn Féin party was split between pro-Treaty TDs, who would form a government for the new state, and the anti-Treaty TDs, who refused to recognise the legitimacy of this state.[3] While Arthur Griffith succeeded de Valera as President of Dáil Éireann on 10 January, after the former resigned in protest over the acceptance of the Treaty, 'the real responsibility for launching the new state on a safe course lay with the Provisional Government, established under the Treaty … for a maximum period of one year with Collins as chairman'.[4]

Serious obstacles confronted Collins in his new capacity as chairman of the Provisional Government. Apart from the issues of raising finance and reorganising the civil service, Collins sought unsuccessfully to reconcile political differences with the anti-Treaty TDs. As uncertainty prevailed, anti-Treaty IRA factions attempted to reignite the War of Independence by carrying out eighty-two attacks on RIC personnel, leading to twelve deaths and twenty-two men being seriously wounded between December 1921 and February 1922.[5] In the southern half of the country, a spate of fatal attacks on RIC men occurred during the first two weeks of February, resulting in the deaths of Constable Charles Ednie in Killarney, County Kerry; Constables William Gorlay and Frank Kershaw in Lisdoonvara, County Clare; District Inspector Michael Keany in Clonakilty, County Cork; and Constable Lauchlin McEdward in Garryowen, County Limerick.[6] In response to this state of lawlessness and the renewed violence against a force preparing for disbandment, *The Irish Times* publicly questioned the Provisional Government's intentions regarding the establishment of a much-needed police force.[7] In response to the attacks, the RIC remained in barracks during the early months of 1922 awaiting formal disbandment.

THE ORGANISING COMMITTEE

In February 1922 arrangements for the formation of a new police force began in earnest. Responsibility for the proposed force came under the remit of the minister for home affairs, Éamonn Duggan. Before entering politics, Duggan, himself the son of an RIC man, had qualified as a solicitor, fought in the Easter Rising of 1916 and briefly held the senior position of director of intelligence in the IRA. Duggan had accompanied Collins as one of the five envoys appointed to negotiate a treaty with the British government in 1921, and later signed the Anglo-Irish Treaty in London in the Irish delegation's headquarters at Hans Place, Knightsbridge. With the deterioration of the political situation and the seeming inevitability of civil war, Collins established an 'organising committee', composed primarily of his own former police agents and loyal IRA officers who had assisted him during the War of Independence. The primary function of this organising committee was to help Duggan establish a replacement police force for the RIC.

The most notable appointments made by Collins to the committee were two serving RIC district inspectors, Patrick Walsh and John A. Kearney. Collins was eager to draw on their expertise and was assured by his own sources that both men had demonstrated nationalist sympathies during the War of Independence.[8] Walsh was stationed in Letterkenny Barracks in County Donegal. He had completed thirty years' service in the RIC. Kearney had completed three years of training as a Christian Brother before embarking on a career in the RIC and, following successive promotions, was stationed at Boyle in County Roscommon. On 3 February 1922, Collins wrote to Walsh and Kearney, inviting them to become members of the organising committee, which would hold its inaugural meeting at the Gresham Hotel in Dublin on 9 February. In his letter to both men, Collins stated the intention of the Provisional Government to create a committee with 'the purpose of drafting a scheme for the organisation of a new Police Force'.[9] Collins attended the first meeting and was accompanied by the minister for home affairs, Éamonn Duggan, and the minister for defence, General Richard Mulcahy, as well as a selection of high-profile IRA men including Brigadier Michael Joseph Ring (County Mayo), Colonel Patrick Brennan TD (County Clare), Commandant Martin Lynch (County Laois), and Divisional Adjutant P. J. Haugh (County Clare). The IRA was also represented by intelligence officer Jeremiah Maher (County Kildare), who had been an RIC sergeant until July 1920.[10] Three district inspectors – Walsh, Kearney and Thomas McGettrick (Howth) – represented the personnel of the RIC. Sergeants Patrick Harte (County Inspector's Office, Roscommon), Mathias McCarthy (Belfast), Edmond Prendiville (Clonmel), Michael McCormack (Letterkenny), John Galligan (Carrick-on-Shannon) and Head Constable James Brennan (RIC depot) also accompanied them. Inspector Michael Kelly (DMP, Donnybrook), Constable Thomas Neary (DMP, Kevin Street) and former Detective Sergeant Edward Broy, who had provided Collins with highly confidential information while employed as a DMP clerk in Dublin Castle during the War of Independence, represented the DMP.[11] Broy went on to be appointed as commissioner of An Garda Síochána in 1933. The committee was heavily dependent on the professional expertise of the DMP and RIC personnel selected by Collins.

General Mulcahy was originally appointed as chairman of the committee, but because of an increasing workload, he requested that Michael Staines, TD, assume the duties of chairman.[12] A native of Newport, County Mayo, and the son of an RIC man, Staines was a former member of the Supreme

Council of the IRB who had fought in the 1916 Rising. On his release from internment in Frongoch, North Wales, he had served as an alderman in Dublin City Corporation and in the general election of 1918 was returned as a Sinn Féin Member of Parliament in the Dublin constituency of St Michan's. During the War of Independence he had acted in a variety of roles on the instruction of Collins. In 1920 Staines organised the Belfast Boycott, which involved a campaign against the purchase of goods and services from unionist-owned companies and banks in the city of Belfast. While the intention was to demonstrate the economic reality of partition, the boycott arguably reinforced the notion that Ireland was now fundamentally two separate states. Before the Belfast endeavour Staines had served as a Republican Police liaison officer in Galway and had furnished Collins with a report on the conditions inside the Rath Internment Camp in County Kildare, which held IRA prisoners.[13]

Collins informed Staines that the RIC would be disbanded on 20 February 1922 and that he and his committee would have a mere three weeks to arrange for the establishment and recruitment of the replacement force.[14] Under the direction of Staines, sub-committees were formed to expedite the drafting of a report for the establishment of the force under such headings as Organisation, Recruitment, Training, and Conditions of Service. After three weeks of intensive discussions and drafting, the report of the organising committee was forwarded to the Provisional Government for consideration. The fundamental recommendations of the committee proposed that the new force would be established on similar lines to the RIC. Each member would be armed with a Webley revolver, but the maximum number of men employed by the new force would be in the region of 4,300, approximately half the number who had served in the RIC. The organisation and the training of the force would follow the RIC format, to the extent that the latter's training manuals of instruction were recommended for use by the new force.[15]

While the organising committee completed its task of furnishing the Provisional Government with a blueprint for the proposed force, the three-week time constraint proved detrimental to the establishment of the Civic Guard for a variety of reasons. First, Collins impetuously attempted to accelerate proceedings by imposing his own selection of RIC, DMP and IRA personnel on the organising committee. These men generally perceived their selection by Collins to be a reward for their service during the War of Independence, and they concentrated on seeking favourable positions in the new force. Second, the lack of available time obliged the committee to be pragmatic and heavily reliant on members who possessed police experience. Consequently, the ex-RIC members of the committee promoted the continued use of the RIC model of training and recommended that the Civic Guard be essentially modelled on the RIC. Third, the unique composition of the committee as selected by Collins led to a series of compromises between parties with conflicting ideologies. Hence, potential IRA recruits were to be granted first preference as members of the new force, while dismissed or resigned RIC and DMP men who had proven patriotic credentials were to be given second preference. Applications from former members of the RIC and DMP would require verification from local IRA officers. Their years of service were to be recognised generously under the new arrangements:

> Members of the Old Force who are taken into the New Force will have the number of years service in the Old Force counted towards pay and pension as if they had served from the date of their joining the Old Force and they be given the rank for which they are considered qualified having regard to their former status, records and fitness for command.[16]

Such policies demonstrated a bizarre lack of foresight by the organising committee, as it failed to anticipate the degree of suspicion and resentment among ex-IRA men towards former RIC men. From the outset, the force was doomed by the recommendations to fill the force with pro-Treaty IRA men and to provide higher rates of pay for ex-RIC men recruited to the force. In addition, the committee was unrealistic in the expectation that a police force replicating the structure of the RIC could attain the necessary goodwill of a public that was expecting an inevitable civil war. The mood of the country demanded the *replacement* of the RIC, rather than the enshrinement of it.[17]

IRELAND'S FIRST NATIONAL POLICE FORCE

On 17 February 1922, the Provisional Government received the report of the organising committee. It was proposed that the Civic Guard would follow the DMP's example of promoting men exclusively within its own ranks. The criteria for selecting the first recruits were similar to those previously used by the RIC. Each member was to be at least 5 ft 9 in (1.75 metres) tall, unmarried and between the ages of 19 and 27.[18] The educational entrance standards of the new force were also similar to RIC and DMP regulations:

> Reading, writing from dictation, spelling and arithmetic – the first four rules simple and compound. They will be asked to write a short composition on a simple subject, either as a letter or statement … Any candidate failing to secure one third of the marks in those subjects, or whose literary qualifications are obviously inferior, will be rejected.[19]

The organising committee recommended the establishment of temporary recruitment stations on a national basis. Within the confines of recruitment stations, the suitability of candidates was to be assessed in terms of literary ability and physique. On admission to the force, recruits would be required to complete a six-month training course, throughout which they would follow the two-hour 'Police Duties' class that was synonymous with the Phoenix Park training regime. The new recruits would also be obliged to complete an additional one-hour class in the Irish language. On completion of three hours of classes, the daily routine was also to include three hours of drill and gymnasium instruction under the supervision of ex-RIC, DMP or IRA personnel. It was proposed by the committee that, after six months of training, recruits would be required to display a satisfactory knowledge of police duties and sufficient fluency in Irish before they would be permitted to enter the police service. The committee concluded its report by identifying the RIC Training Manual as the appropriate text for training recruits. It recommended that 'with necessary deletions and alterations [the manual] could be utilised for some time'.[20]

Within four days of receiving the report of the committee, the Provisional Government accepted its proposals and authorised the immediate commencement of recruitment under the acting commissionership of Michael Staines. Because of the political sensitivities prevailing in February 1922, Staines was not permitted to place public advertisements in the newspapers; instead, the initial recruitment process involved him secretively issuing a circular letter to a selection of IRA brigade officers, requesting the immediate allocation of suitable men to the temporarily acquired headquarters of the Civic Guard at the Royal Dublin Society (RDS), Ballsbridge, Dublin. The facilities at the RDS required minimum alterations, as the British army had been occupying the premises for the latter part of the War of Independence.[21] In an effort to hasten the recruitment process, appointment officers were employed temporarily in each of the twelve recruitment stations between February and July 1922.[22] Their primary duty was to ensure that the prospective recruits satisfied the physical and educational standards set by the organising committee.

TRAINING BEHIND CLOSED DOORS

Controversy surrounds the identity of the first man recruited to the Civic Guard. On 21 February 1922, Patrick McAvinia was officially registered as the first recruit, but within the first week, P. J. Kerrigan was provided with the registration of No. 1, on the basis that he had arrived at the RDS before McAvinia. Six months later, Kerrigan was dismissed from the force for striking a prisoner.[23] Both men were of RIC origin. Similarly, on 27 February, a former RIC district inspector, Bernard O'Connor, was appointed as the receiving and measuring officer, with responsibility for ensuring the official enlistment of all recruits.[24] On 8 March national newspapers published reports that the Civic Guard had been established. Readers were informed that the bulk of the force would be recruited from within the IRA and the remainder from the RIC. It was also noted that the former policemen would constitute 'a fair proportion of men who were formerly in the Royal Irish Constabulary, but resigned in sympathy with the Sinn Féin movement'.[25] Two days later, the public was informed by *The Irish Times* of the criteria for recruitment and the rates of payment for the lower ranks:

THE IRISH CIVIC GUARD: Recruiting for the National Civic Guard which has its temporary headquarters at the Royal Dublin Society's premises at Ballsbridge, is proceeding rapidly. Recruits, who are arriving daily from all parts of the country, are required to be at least 5ft. 9in. in height, and must have a mean chest measurement of 36 inches. The age is between 19 and 27 years. The pay of a constable will start at 70s. a week, and that of a sergeant at 100s. Appointment stations have been established at various centres. The design and colour of the uniforms have not yet been decided. The design will probably be similar to the IRA uniform, and the colour will probably be a bluish-grey. The members, who are mostly members of the IRA, are being trained by ex-members of the Royal Irish Constabulary, under the command of Commandant P. Brennan TD.[26]

Despite the early enlistment of former RIC men at the RDS, approximately ninety-four per cent of the first 1,250 recruits registered by O'Connor were of IRA origin.[27] The remaining six per cent were of RIC origin, of whom half had resigned from that organisation and joined the IRA.

In his account of the early days of the Civic Guard, ex-sergeant Patrick Campbell of County Galway recalls his arrival at the Ballsbridge training headquarters. Only weeks before his enlistment, Campbell had been an active member of the Western Division of the IRA. His superior officer informed him that a new police force was soon to be established and that he should make immediate application. Campbell recalls the circumstances of his recruitment:

It was arranged for about 12 men to sit an examination at Lenaboy Castle, where other candidates were being attested. Having succeeded at the examination, I with other successful candidates was instructed to return to our homes [sic] and procure references from our Parish Priest and local Volunteer commander. In the course of a few days I received a calling up notice to report at Ballsbridge Training Centre on 25 March 1922 and that transport would meet me at Broadstone Railway Station. I entrained at Ballinasloe Railway Station on 25 March 1922 and joined a number of boys from Oranmore who were also going to Ballsbridge. At Ballsbridge we were unloaded outside and entered the Receiving Office where our arrival was recorded and I learned that I was the 480th member to register and that the name of the force that I had joined was the Civic Guard. The entire party of the latest 'Rookies' were then guided out to the horse stalls in the Enclosure. Each man was handed an empty mattress cover made of stiff canvas. Each candidate was directed to fill his mattress with straw from the stalls, then back to the Main Hall where we laid our mattress on 3 boards stretched on 2 wooden trestles and standing about 6 inches from the floor, there were about 1,000 men so accommodated on the floor of the vast hall and surrounding balconies.[28]

The selection of the RDS as the temporary headquarters of the Civic Guard proved wholly unsuitable for the training of recruits. The director of the RDS, Edward Bohane, informed Minister Duggan that facilities could only be extended for a period of less than two months, as they needed to prepare for the forthcoming annual Spring Show.[29] The establishment of the Civic Guard was further hindered by a shortage of instructors to train recruits in the cramped surroundings and ill-equipped venue. Six ex-RIC instructors were appointed to provide instruction in drill and classes in police studies. Former members of the force recall that a typical day at the RDS began with reveille at 6.30 a.m. Recruits were given one hour to themselves before breakfast. After that, recruits completed drill and prepared their uniforms and dormitories for inspection. At 8.45 a.m. they attended morning parade, which was followed by an additional session of drill.[30] After dinner was served at 1 p.m., recruits were occupied with lessons in police duties, Irish language and physical training until tea at 5 p.m. Despite the classes being held in police duties and the Irish language, the curriculum was considered disjointed and sporadic because of the lack of instructors and classrooms.[31] After tea, recruits were permitted to leave the grounds of the RDS until roll call. However, each night brought its quota of accidents as a result of the 'country boys jumping off moving trams outside the buildings when rushing back for roll call at 10 p.m.'[32]

On 11 March 1922, Michael Staines was officially appointed commissioner of the Civic Guards. He later stated that he had intended to complete only three months in his new role, as he had little interest in continuing the position on a long-term basis.[33] The government controlled the selection of the headquarters staff and Staines was not consulted about the appointments. During the month of March, members of the organising committee and former loyal IRA, DMP and RIC agents of Collins effectively jockeyed for high-ranking positions. Consequently, an anomalous mixture of individuals entered the RDS and awaited a favourable appointment.

In addition to the various factions seeking preferment, it was also significant that Staines and two other senior members of the Civic Guard were serving members of the

Provisional Government. The two elected representatives from County Clare had a significant influence on the composition and future of the Civic Guard. Seán Liddy, TD, was a former IRA brigade officer and was appointed to the rank of superintendent.[34] During the War of Independence, members of the RIC in County Clare had been ordered to shoot Liddy on sight.[35] Patrick Brennan, TD, was a former IRA colonel commandant and brother to Michael and Austin Brennan, who between them effectively controlled the East Clare IRA battalion. Born in 1893, Brennan was the eldest child of a farmer from Meelick in County Clare. By 1915 he had moved temporarily to work in London and had joined the IRB. In preparation for the 1916 Rising, Brennan was sent to Carrigaholt in County Clare to collect boats for 'the transhipment of the arms' from the ill-fated *Aud* at Banna Beach, County Kerry, and was to land the arms in Kilrush, County Clare, 'where he was to have trains ready to move arms through Ennis and up to Galway'.[36] Following the Rising, Brennan and his brother Michael were sent to the internment camp at Frongoch. On his return to Ireland, Brennan was appointed IRA brigadier for County Clare, but later resigned, citing as his reason interference from general headquarters. Following his departure, the IRA divided County Clare into three battalions and Brennan served temporarily under the command of his brother Michael in the East Clare Battalion.[37] Following Brennan's involvement in organising security for Sinn Féin representatives at elections throughout the country, he was returned in the general election of 1921 as a TD in

County Clare alongside his fellow Sinn Féin colleagues, Seán Liddy, Éamon de Valera and Brian O'Higgins. In March 1922, he was selected by the organising committee as the depot commandant of the Civic Guard. In the weeks before his call to the RDS, Brennan had already undertaken the role of chief appointment officer and supervised a team of appointment officers as they enlisted potential recruits on a national basis.

Brennan later recalled the difficulties of recruiting IRA men in particular counties where anti-Treaty IRA officers resented the fact that officers were travelling around the country meeting pro-Treaty IRA brigade officers to identify suitable members for the new force: 'We got appointment officers in Clare, Galway and other counties. In various counties like Cork, Kerry, Mayo, we could not get appointment officers, or if we sent them, they were arrested' and detained because of their loyalty to the Provisional Government. According to Brennan, the former IRA Brigadier M. J. Ring was appointment officer in his native county of Mayo when he was detained:

> and had to go on hunger strike to get out. [Daniel] Hallinan was arrested in Cork. We had difficulties to contend with. The appointment officer went around or went to Volunteer Companies and got men from each Company. He put these through an examination in reading, writing and arithmetic. He also got them examined by a doctor, and sent them on.[38]

The appointment of the six ex-RIC instructors as advisers to the Civic Guard during March proved to be the first of many controversial decisions that destabilised the embryonic force. In his recollection, Liddy claims that the appointment of ex-RIC personnel to positions above the rank and file generated resentment among his former IRA comrades in the RDS. Though he accepted that Collins was merely demonstrating his gratitude to the RIC men for their assistance as agents during the War of Independence, he empathised with the IRA recruits in the Civic Guard, who 'regarded the RIC as their most bitter antagonists and it little mattered to them if the whole Provisional Government, or any individual members of it, thought they owed a debt of gratitude to certain individuals of that now defunct and disbanded force'.[39] Tensions between recruits and newly appointed ex-RIC officers were also strained by the refusal of the men to salute the former RIC men. The unavailability of uniforms had facilitated such a practice, so distinctive coloured armbands were issued to identify the ranks of sergeant, inspector and superintendent.[40] However, many of the recruits still refused to salute ex-RIC men.

While Liddy and other members of the Civic Guard were annoyed by the admittance of former RIC members to the force, they were unaware that the minister for local government, W. T. Cosgrave, had in January received a handwritten request from the former commanding officer of the Auxiliaries, Brigadier General Crozier, asking Cosgrave to assist him in attaining a commissioned position in the new police force: 'Dear Sir, if you have an opportunity will you use your influence, in the event of a settlement, to get me an Executive appointment under the new Govt. in Ireland? If you could, I would be very grateful. My record, I consider, shows work in the benefit of Ireland, to my own loss and of my family [*sic*].'[41] Thereafter, Crozier took it upon himself to write regularly to the minister for home affairs, Éamonn Duggan, and even suggested that he had earned a commissioned rank in the Civic Guard in recognition of his decision, as commanding officer of the Auxiliaries during the War of Independence, to resign his position in protest at the reinstatement of some of his men despite their part in looting and other unlawful acts. The Department of Home Affairs replied that they would hold his application on file and that Duggan was 'too busy' to meet with Crozier.[42]

In late February, tensions mounted within the RDS as the rumour circulated that former RIC District Inspector John Kearney was to be appointed to the position of deputy commissioner, making him second in command to Staines. The streets of Ballsbridge were the source of rumours, as anti-Treaty republicans distributed posters and handbills to passing recruits, claiming that Kearney and other RIC men were to attain senior positions in the Civic Guard.[43] Kearney, a member of the organising committee, drew the particular attention of the Kerry recruits and the anti-Treaty republicans in Ballsbridge, as he was identified as the head constable responsible for the arrest of Sir Roger Casement on Banna Beach in County Kerry before the 1916 Easter Rising. The resentment of recruits towards Kearney was probably intensified by comments voiced in Dáil Éireann on 28 February 1922. During exchanges between deputies, the anti-Treaty IRA commandant, Austin Stack, TD, whom Kearney had previously arrested in Tralee Barracks, raised serious objections to the presence of Kearney at the Civic Guard depot:[44]

> This man Kearney was, from my experience of him, one of the most vigilant servants the enemy had in this country, and he did his best – by open means and underhand – to beat us. He claimed to have been the means of preventing the Rising in Kerry in 1916, and, I suppose, persuaded his superiors that such was the case, because to my own knowledge, he was a man who had previously failed in all his examinations for promotion to the position of District Inspector. In consequence of what he did in 1916 he received the promotion. He remained in the R.I.C. during the whole period of the war and, in common with others in the R.I.C., he did not resign when called upon by the country. Instead of recognition, he deserves from the Dáil – or any other people's Government in this country – reprobation.[45]

Liddy described the feelings of resentment towards Kearney among the recruits and claimed that plans were afoot to remove the former district inspector from the grounds of the RDS:

> The Kerry Lads denounced Kearney as Casement's betrayer and executioner to all and sundry within the camp. This news had an electrifying effect on all the IRA men, producing an explosive force equal to 1,500 lbs. of T.N.T., ready to explode with violent eruption at any moment. An air of high velocity tension pervaded the camp; in their spare moments groups of men could be seen engaged in earnest discussion; at night time meetings were held in the main hall where the men dined and slept.[46]

THE 'PROTEST COMMITTEE'

Such feelings of discontent led to the establishment of an estimated fourteen-man protest committee largely composed of
IRA column men who, because of their particular experience
in firearms, had been selected as the Special Guard for sentry
duties.[47] The leading men of this committee included Guards
Byrne, Kilroy, Hennessy, O'Meara, O'Halloran, Branigan,
Diggans and Coy.[48] According to Guard John O'Meara, he
and his fellow East Limerick IRA comrades who had joined
the Civic Guard were so appalled by the appointment of
former RIC members to the force that they fully intended
to resign, and arranged a meeting with Liam Hayes, TD, to
discuss the matter. Hayes had been their brigade commandant in the IRA: 'We told him it was full of RIC, that they
held every commission and every rank in it, and that we were
not going to serve under them, that if we were going to serve
them we could not respect them as officers, that I for one,
would not salute them, that the hand would rot off me first.'[49]
Following a meeting with the commissioner in Ballsbridge,
Hayes returned to the men and assured them that the appointments were of a temporary nature.[50] Similarly, Guard
Patrick Coy, a former captain in the East Galway brigade of
the IRA, recalled on his arrival the uneasy atmosphere within
the depot and the subsequent establishment of the protest
committee:

> About 50 others with me joined the Civic Guard on 4 March.
> During hours of recreation we met pals out of the city in the

evenings and had several conversations with them, and with the men in the depot also. Our letters from home from our pals told us that we would be an unrecognised body in the country by joining Collins' Tans, as we had done, and selling the principle that we fought the last seven years for. We told them that we were prepared to place these facts before the government at the first opportunity we could get. We told the men then that the only way out of the grievance was to place those facts in writing before the commandant of the depot.[51]

On 14 March, Commandant Brennan was requested to forward a document to the Provisional Government signed by the secretary of the protest committee, Guard Matthew Diggans, on behalf of the members. The document essentially set out grievances and recommendations regarding the employment of ex-RIC and ex-DMP personnel in the Civic Guard:

… we have competent IRA Officers here that are in every way capable of training us in any way that we may require since they trained us to fight the common enemy, England, under terrible difficulties, and I may also add to fight the majority of the RIC.

That members of the late RIC and DMP must not be allowed to cater for us in the cook-houses or in any way have authority whatsoever over us in future.

That members of the late RIC and DMP must not be supplied with better sleeping accommodation or better food than what we have.

That ex-RIC and ex-DMP should not retain their rank and service attained during the rule of the Saxon while there are IRA men here that have given four and five years' service free to their country and they are quite satisfied to loose [*sic*] both rank and service.

That all recruiting for the Irish Civic Guard must be from the ranks of the IRA first as stated in the *Irish Independent* 7th inst, and that under no circumstances will we tolerate the disbanded RIC in here that bore arms for the enemy up to the present day to suppress the National instinct of the Irish people.

That we are satisfied to work with ex-RIC that resigned on principle and proved the sincerity of their principle by taking up their arms and fought with their brothers for the common cause, provided that such members can tell us what and where they fought and who was their O/C [Officer Commanding].

That we know several members of the IRA that were in active service during the war and who are both physically and mentally fit for the Civic Guard if it was worked on a proper basis.

That since we came into this Depot our very best friends refuse to recognise us since we degraded ourselves so much as to be associated with such dreadful characters as the RIC.[52]

On the day that the protest committee presented Brennan with the document, Sergeant Thomas Kilroy recalled, 'We explained to the commandant that the men were refusing to parade, whilst those members of the RIC were in the Camp.'[53] Kilroy, a former company captain in the IRA, held a personal disdain for the RIC. During the War of Independence he had been arrested by members of the RIC and beaten to such an extent that he was unconscious for twenty-two days. He later served fourteen months of his sentence of penal servitude for life.[54] According to Brennan, Kilroy and other members of the committee informed him that there would be a mass 'walk-out of the depot if the RIC men were not hunted out'.[55] Their immediate demands were twofold: first, the immediate removal of Kearney; and second, the removal of disbanded RIC personnel holding commissioned rank in the Civic Guards.[56]

Brennan was well regarded by the recruits as a result of his exploits as the former East Clare IRA colonel commandant. As one of the few ex-IRA men to attain a senior position on the Civic Guard headquarters staff, his clarification on the issue was eagerly sought by the committee. On reading the document, Brennan initially agreed to forward it to the government. However, unknown to the protest committee, he subsequently decided not to send it on as, 'I felt it was a small squabble and that it should not go beyond us, if we could fix it.'[57] According to Brennan, the recruits at this time were paranoid about being associated with members of the RIC and were anxious that the training of the force would be conducted exclusively by their former enemies: 'There were a hundred different things. RIC used to come in there and they felt that should not be … Every RIC man that came in could not be training the Civic Guard. There were all kinds of small troubles we had to guard against, and I had a fairly hot time.'[58] Brennan allayed the anxieties of the committee temporarily by reiterating Liam Hayes' earlier assertion that the employment of RIC 'advisers' was a temporary arrangement.[59] According to Kilroy, 'He told us that he was led to believe that those men were only there temporarily, and when the constitution of the Civic Guard would be formed that those men's services would be dispensed with. That satisfied the men and things went on smoothly.'[60] On concluding the meeting with the protest committee, Brennan advised Commissioner Staines of the demand for the removal of Kearney from the force.

On 21 March Staines arranged a meeting with his government colleagues, Minister Duggan and minister for publicity, Desmond Fitzgerald.[61] They discussed the anti-Treaty campaign that had been designed to persuade the public that ex-RIC personnel would effectively take charge of the Civic Guard. The campaign had contributed to the establishment of the protest committee and its objections to Kearney and other RIC instructors in the depot. During the meeting it was agreed that Fitzgerald would seek clarification from IRA officers in County Roscommon about Kearney's relationship with the local IRA brigade. It was also arranged that a press statement would be issued on behalf of the Provisional Government, which would disprove anti-Treaty claims that the force was appointing RIC men to senior positions within the Civic Guard. On 25 March *The Irish Times* and the *Irish Independent* published the Provisional Government's rebuttal under the respective headings of 'All IRA Men Except 30' and 'The Civic Guard Falsehood Refuted'. The statement was brief and succinct:

False statements are being assiduously circulated through the country with regard to the Civic Guard. It is asserted that the Guard is largely composed of Black and Tans. The facts are as follows:- The present strength of the Civic Guard is 400. Of these, 370 are members of the IRA and 30 are resigned RIC men. Of these 30, about 25 did war service in the ranks of the IRA, in the active service columns and in other capacities ... All officers of the Civic Guard so far appointed are IRA men ... Commandant Patrick Brennan, East Clare, ASU, IRA; Captain P. Haugh, West Clare IRA, Comdt. M. Ring, Commander West Mayo, ASU, IRA and Comdt. M. Lynch, Brigade Police Officer, Leix, IRA. There are no Black and Tans in the Civic Guard.[62]

The publication of the statement occurred the day before the convention of the Irish Republican Army was to be held at the Mansion House in Dublin city. Despite the anti-Treaty IRA convention being outlawed by the Provisional Government, the meeting was attended by 220 delegates representing forty-nine brigades, who were protected inside the building by armed men, while, much to the annoyance of the organisers, 'it was noted that armed parties of the Civic Guard were on duty in the street [Dawson Street]'.[63] The primary purpose of the anti-Treaty IRA convention was to repudiate the authority of the Provisional Government, establish its own Army Executive Council of sixteen men and to claim responsibility for the governance of the Irish people until such time that complete independence for Ireland was achieved. During the convention, the delegates passed a motion which ordered 'all officers and other ranks at present serving in the "Regular" Army, and members of the Civic Guard, to return to their respective units, and that recruiting for these forces shall cease forthwith'.[64] A report on the convention, published in *The Irish Times,* noted that 'a clash between the authority of the Dáil Éireann Defence Ministry and the [anti-Treaty IRA] "Executive Council" can hardly be avoided'.[65]

On 27 March, two days after the publication of the government's statement denying the rumours that former RIC men had been appointed to senior positions in the Civic Guard, Staines sought to allay further the anxieties of the protesting recruits by announcing the promotion of Commandant Brennan to the position of assistant commissioner. This placed him below just Staines and the deputy commissioner in rank. On receiving notice of his promotion, Brennan informed Staines that he did not wish to take up the appointment and 'asked him to place Mr Ring in the place of assistant commissioner'.[66] However, in spite of his efforts to remain as commandant of the depot, Brennan was eventually persuaded by Staines to take the position of assistant commissioner.

Moreover, despite the publication of the rebuttal, Staines subsequently informed Kearney of the difficulties surrounding his temporary employment in the depot and 'seeing that there was no likelihood of a future for him in the new force, and fearing for his own personal safety, he left Ballsbridge depot, taking the mail boat to England and travelling on to London'.[67] Following his exile to London, Kearney and his family took up permanent residence in England. Though temporary relief among the force followed Kearney's departure, Staines' efforts to placate the protest committee through the removal of Kearney and the promotion of Brennan arguably undermined the commissioner's authority and raised the profile of the protestors among the rank and file. On examining the career of Kearney, one must question whether the Kerry recruits were so oblivious to the contribution of the former RIC district inspector to the IRA campaign, or whether disgruntled IRA officers in the Civic Guard allowed themselves to be manipulated by the committee. Following the transportation of Roger Casement from Banna Beach to the Tralee RIC Barracks, Kearney had demonstrated his patriotism by establishing a strong rapport with Casement, leaving the barrack door open and warning his wife that he expected local Volunteers to enter the barracks later in the night to rescue the prisoner.[68] With regard to Kearney's arrest of Austin Stack, Staines claimed that it was unavoidable, as the IRA man entered the RIC barracks in Tralee:

> when Kearney had an order for his arrest in his pocket. There were five or six other policemen there when Austin Stack went into the Barracks, and he arrested him. But I would like to make it plain to everybody that Kearney was not an officer of the Civic Guard. He was a member of the organising committee and he was appointed by the Provisional Government, not by me. When it came to the question of appointing officers I sacked Kearney.[69]

Unfortunately for Kearney, the intelligence information requested by Minister Fitzgerald about the district inspector's treatment of the local IRA brigade in County Roscommon only became available three months later. The handwritten attestation of the North Roscommon IRA intelligence officer, Padraig Ó Dubhaoinrigh, confirmed that Kearney assisted the

IRA on a number of occasions during his placement in Boyle, County Roscommon: 'As Brigade I.O. for North Roscommon I am in a position to give some idea how Mr Carney [*sic*], DI, Boyle, helped me during the fight … Carney on one occasion reported to us that a certain house in the 1st Batt. Area was to be raided.' Ó Dubhaoinrigh explains that the house was frequented by two IRA men whom, he claims, would have been shot by the police if the subsequent raid had proved successful. In a similar occurrence, Ó Dubhaoinrigh recounts that Kearney informed him that the Auxiliaries intended shooting seven men in the North Roscommon area: 'I was one of them. Mr Carney [*sic*] sent us word to clear out … We left our homes and some nights later, four of the men to be shot were raided by the Auxiliaries. When all danger was over, Mr Carney sent us word that we could return to our homes again.' In his concluding remarks, Ó Dubhaoinrigh testifies that Kearney personally provided him with ammunition, and that 'he saved several of our men from being shot after arrest'.[70]

In stark contrast to the testimony offered by the IRA officer, historian Pádraig Óg Ó Ruairc has recently unearthed the unpublished memoirs of Lieutenant Colonel Trollope of the British army (Essex Regiment), who served in Boyle during the War of Independence. According to Trollope, Kearney successfully endeared himself to the locals but had fully convinced the British army officer of his loyalty to the crown:

> Boyle itself was entirely peaceful under the rule of the District Inspector of Irish Constabulary, Kearney. He was entirely loyal

to the crown and his Oath of Allegiance, he made no mistake about arresting any Irishman he knew was a danger to the public, but he was always just to those whom he felt were at heart decent fellows and were only misled by the fanatics. There were not many of them. He should have been the best hated man in the district whose life was not worth insuring, but in spite of an order from the Irish Constabulary Headquarters that all police must sleep in the police barracks, he always slept at his private house, a good half mile from the barracks ... His best story was the arrest of Sir Roger Casement in 1916 ... instead of a local and stupid policeman, he [Casement] was up against Kearney who hunted and found him hiding in a disused barn on the coast where he was hiding.[71]

The Appointment of District Inspector Walsh

In the wake of Kearney's abrupt departure, Staines agreed to Brennan's request to allow him to meet the protest committee and to ask them to provide him with the names of IRA men they would consider as suitable replacements for the RIC instructors at the depot:

They said, for example, that they had plenty of men who could teach police duties. I asked them to give me their names and they could not. They gave them to me afterwards. I sent these men out and found that they were not much use until we trained them. I put it to them as I was more or less directed, that you could not train a police force without the assistance of some kind of police. There were a number of things such as execution of warrants, inquests, and other things that the RIC were accustomed to deal with. They said they would object to certain RIC men, but they would not object to others.[72]

During April the number of recruits continued to swell until there were more than 1,000. Gradually, a system of organised training was imposed. On 6 April, less than two weeks after the Provisional Government published its statement declaring that only IRA men had been appointed to officer positions within the Civic Guard, the most significant contributor of the organising committee, former RIC District Inspector Patrick Walsh, was officially appointed as deputy commissioner. The appointment was convenient for Walsh, as he had been demobilised from the RIC just the day before he was officially unveiled as deputy commissioner. The undoubted talent and zeal of Walsh soon permeated the RDS grounds. The division of men into eight companies and adherence to a timetable of drills and classes provided a regulated structure.[73]

The newly appointed deputy commissioner was not without his critics, however. Liddy asserted that Walsh effectively usurped Staines in almost every aspect of his commissioner-ship, to the extent that Walsh introduced a training regime that was 'a replica of the old, the RIC Code (or as some of the boys jocosely referred to it as [sic] the "Devil's prayer book").'[74] Though Liddy described Staines as 'a perfectly honest man', he criticised the commissioner for allowing Walsh to impose an alleged RIC ethos on the force. In addition, he claimed that Staines was too loyal to Collins and allowed the chairman of the Provisional Government to appoint his 'pets' to positions of power in the Civic Guard. According to Liddy, the newly appointed assistant commissioner, Patrick Brennan, was the only senior officer to oppose Walsh's quest to establish a force on the lines of the RIC, but was 'no match in the diplomatic battlefield for the astute Walsh'.[75]

On the same day as Walsh's appointment, Commandant Seán Broderick of the National Army issued a press statement regarding the capture of the Civic Guard's recruitment centre at Lenaboy Castle, outside Galway city, by anti-Treaty forces and explained the Executive Council's determination to compel the disbandment of the Civic Guard. In his statement, Broderick announced that the 'Irregular' (anti-Treaty) soldiers holding Lenaboy Castle were in possession of important Civic Guard documents, and that recruitment to the force in County Galway would be suspended temporarily.[76] It was later reported that on the same evening a number of men arrived at the home of the Barrett family in Skreen, County Sligo. Following a knock at his door, Mr Barrett was asked by the men to call his son, who had earlier received news that he had been successful in his application to join the Civic Guard. On hearing the commotion at the door, Mr Barrett's son attempted to evade the men but was shot in the head and 'removed to a Dublin hospital'.[77]

OCCUPATION OF THE FOUR COURTS
As Walsh continued with the imposition of a new order in the RDS, the recruits became increasingly worried by the unwanted attention of anti-Treaty units, which engaged in

nightly sniper fire on the camp.[78] The hostility directed by the anti-Treaty men towards their former comrades in the RDS was soon overshadowed by events less than three miles from the headquarters of the Civic Guard. On 14 April 1922, the chairman of the Army Executive, Rory O'Connor, led anti-Treaty troops into the Four Courts, the centre of the Irish judiciary, and seized the building. On the same day, Liam Mellows, secretary to the Army Executive, wrote to the secretary of Dáil Éireann on behalf of the 'Irregulars' and proposed six conditions to prevent civil war. One of the conditions required the Provisional Government to disband the Civic Guard: 'the policing of the country to be carried out by the Irish Republican Army, as decided by the Executive of that Army'.[79] In an interview with a journalist on the same day, O'Connor informed the Irish public that his forces were 'altogether opposed to the Civic Guard' and that 'there was no necessity for its existence, and that it contained Black and Tans'.[80]

The symbolic occupation of the Four Courts challenged the legitimacy of the Provisional Government. In a desperate attempt to avert civil war, Collins chose to ignore the provocative gesture for over two months and instead sought an electoral pact with de Valera for the forthcoming general election in June.

Within the Civic Guard camp, an anti-Treaty faction, under the leadership of a former County Cork IRA officer, Thomas Daly, secretly awaited an opportune moment to unleash havoc within the new force. Following the occupation of the Four Courts, Daly gradually sought the support of his fellow dissident recruits as he prepared to assume leadership of the protest committee with the assistance of former County Galway IRA Vice-Commandant, Patrick Sellars. However, Sellars was unaware that Daly was also the leader of a small number of anti-Treaty Civic Guards who were in communication with Rory O'Connor and who remained alert for instructions from the Four Courts.

As the RDS strained under the large number of recruits, Staines vented his frustration with the Provisional Government. In a letter to the minister for home affairs, Éamonn Duggan, the commissioner informed him that it was 'impossible to maintain any decent standard of discipline ... and if I cannot have possession of the RIC depot within a week, I shall have to hand control to some other person'.[81] However, the remaining RIC personnel refused to leave the Phoenix Park Depot. The matter was further complicated by Edward Bohane's latest reminder that the Civic Guard would have to evacuate the grounds of the RDS to allow preparations for the annual Spring Show.[82] The matter was resolved with the temporary acquisition of the Kildare Artillery Barracks. On 25 April 1922, an estimated 1,100 recruits were transferred to the new headquarters with an arsenal of 200 rifles and 1,000 revolvers.[83] In his recollections as a recruit, John Moore emphasises the fact that they had not been informed by their superiors of plans to transfer the headquarters of the Civic Guard:

> The Show Committee wanted the grounds for the Spring Show, so we had to get out on the next morning. We were told at seven

a.m. to pack up and get ready to move, we were not told where we were going, we boarded a train at a railway station opposite the grounds and arrived at Amiens Street Station and after that the train went through a tunnel, and the first time I knew the direction we were going in was when we were passing by Sallins Station, I remarked to some of the boys we were heading south, being a Leix man I knew the route well, the train stopped at the town of Kildare so we were all told to get out and marched to the Military Barracks, as we were going in, the British military were coming out in lorries and they all waved to us and we returned the salute, they seemed to be glad to be quitting and going for home.[84]

KILDARE ARTILLERY BARRACKS

On their arrival at Kildare Barracks, the accommodation reserved for the recruits needed cleaning, as much of the barracks had previously been used as stables by the British army.[85] Dissatisfaction among the recruits was further exacerbated in early May by the posting of a list of appointments of twelve high commissioned ranks. The majority of the senior vacancies available within the Civic Guard were given to former members of the RIC.[86] Rather than appointing RIC men on a temporary basis, it was apparent that the majority of the influential positions within the force were being reserved for experienced policemen, who were still generally perceived by the recruits as their most bitter enemies. Thomas Daly and his supporters within Kildare Barracks were presented with the opportunity to harness the frustration of the recruits, and a new protest committee was established which comprised fourteen men. Each of the eight companies was allowed to elect two representatives to the committee. However, the men of No. 6 Company declined to select any representatives. The committee members included Daly, Patrick Sellars, Seán O'Brien, E. J. Ryan, Malachy Collison, John Doyle, John O'Meara, Thomas Kilroy and Guards Taylor and Strickland.

The latest list of senior ranking appointments was described by dissident recruits as the proverbial 'straw which broke the camel's back' as it was already 'bad enough to have those ex-RIC "ruling the roost" in civilian capacities. When it came to the pass of giving them high commissions in the Civic Guard, under the authority, and with the consent of the Government, it was felt by the men that a strong protest should be made.'[87]

Personnel appointed to senior Civic Guard ranks, May 1922:[88]

> Michael Staines, TD (ex-IRA), Commissioner
> Patrick Walsh (ex-RIC), Deputy Commissioner
> Patrick Brennan, TD (ex-IRA), Assistant Commissioner
> Chief Superintendent Michael Ring (ex-IRA), Depot Commandant
> Chief Superintendent Mathias McCarthy (ex-RIC), Barrack Master
> Chief Superintendent Michael McCormack (ex-RIC), Accounting Officer
> Superintendent Jeremiah Maher (ex-RIC), Private Secretary
> Superintendent P. J. Haugh (ex-IRA), Adjutant
> Superintendent James Brennan (ex-RIC), Assistant Barrack Master
> Superintendent Patrick Harte (ex-RIC), Assistant Accounting Officer

Superintendent Bernard O'Connor (ex-RIC)
Chief Inspector Robert McCrudden (ex-RIC)

Newly-promoted Assistant Barrack Master James Brennan later recalled the raised tensions within Kildare Barracks following the announcement of the senior appointments in the force. According to Brennan, the Civic Guard had been required to leave the RDS 'on very short notice'. On his arrival at Kildare, he was surprised that 'the place was handed over in a very bad state'. Moreover, he could not find any suitable building to secure the armoury, and within a few days he estimated that dissident recruits had taken, without permission, 400 revolvers and large amounts of ammunition. Brennan, a disbanded RIC head constable who had been a member of the organising committee, was particularly concerned with the issue of the missing revolvers: 'I heard the revolvers would be kept to put us [former RIC men holding commissioned ranks in the Civic Guard] out the gate. I heard that was the reason the revolvers were not handed in.'[89] After Commandant Ring called a General Parade to insist on the return of arms, only ten revolvers remained at large.

STRAINED RELATIONS

As the recruits familiarised themselves with the environs of Kildare Barracks, tensions began to mount between Commissioner Michael Staines and Assistant Commissioner Patrick Brennan. Staines was particularly incensed by Brennan's lack of cordiality towards his new ex-RIC colleagues and accused him of trying to cause divisions between the former IRA and RIC officers by declining to make use of the officers' mess and by taking 'his meals in a different apartment on the grounds that men who were admitted to the Mess were not commissioned Officers. This naturally had some effect on the Junior Officers and led to estrangement.'[90] Brennan conceded that dining in a room beside the officers' mess 'caused a suspicion that I really refused to associate with the RIC'.[91] Though Brennan accepted that he did object to Walsh and other ex-RIC members dining in the officers' mess, he claimed that he objected solely because only officers had the right to enter the officers' mess:

> That is quite right. In every army or police force of the world, the officers' mess is absolutely confined to commissioned Officers, and any other man is not allowed to go into it, and it is a breach of all regulations that I know of anyhow to allow any man other than a commissioned Officer to dine continually in the officers' mess ... There were then Commissioner Staines, myself, Commandant Ring and Superintendent Lynch – those four were the only commissioned Officers I knew of in the Civic Guard. I heard Mr Walsh was [a commissioned officer] the other day. That was the first I knew of that, and if I had known, I would not have objected ... The insinuation in this is that I objected to having ex-members of the RIC in the Mess.

Brennan even claimed that he was unwilling to dine alongside his fellow TD and close IRA comrade, Seán Liddy, in the officers' mess.[92] In contrast to the stance adopted by the former IRA column leader, Walsh later put on record that 'I did not mind what part of the depot I got my meals [in].'[93]

In early May, the deterioration in relations between Staines and Brennan continued as they made arrangements for a Sunday dinner at Kildare Barracks for invited guests, Arthur Griffith, president of Dáil Éireann, his wife and children, and Minister Duggan and his wife. Staines personally drove the Griffiths from their home to Kildare Barracks, while Brennan agreed to drive Minister Duggan and his wife. On the arrival of both cars, Staines was annoyed that Brennan suddenly and 'deliberately absented himself from dinner'.[94] Brennan claimed that he only decided not to dine with the guests on wrongly concluding that only ex-RIC men would join the special guests at dinner. He walked away from the gathering on learning that his ex-IRA comrades were unavailable to dine as they were either attending a football match in Dublin or away on leave: 'On my arrival, I could find no IRA officer except Liddy, and Liddy had had his dinner. What made me suspicious was that every RIC man was present.' Brennan initially believed that Superintendent Edmond Prendiville, the mess caterer, had deliberately ensured that his former RIC comrades had all been invited to the dinner. Brennan later stated that he:

> felt a bit upset that the IRA officers had cleared out because they had not got an invitation of any kind. I say they should have been told. It was a very big affair … it might have been hot temper, but I usually keep my temper on serious occasions, and I did

> walk off because I felt it was an insult to the president and to the
> minister for home affairs, and an insult to our officers there that
> somebody had been guilty of some kind of underhand work ...
> And if the blame is to be placed on anybody it should be on Mr
> Prendiville, because he was the mess caterer.[95]

However, Brennan later admitted that he had made an honest 'misapprehension' about Prendiville's influence and accepted that no ex-RIC were present at the dinner, and that the only guests actually invited to join the Griffiths and Duggans were Staines, Brennan and the doctor at the depot.[96]

In response to the majority of senior positions within the Civic Guard being awarded to former members of the RIC, the protest committee on 12 May circulated a petition among the recruits that sought to demonstrate the level of opposition to the promotion of former RIC men over IRA men. As the petition moved throughout the depot, the committee informed all the recruits that 'the removal of Black and Tans from the camp' was being demanded and that 'if they didn't sign this, Assistant Commissioner Brennan would be dismissed'.[97] Despite no Black and Tans being appointed to the Civic Guard, the protest committee's circulation of the provocative petition consolidated its position as the protector of nationalist ideology among the recruits within the force. Thus a distinct division was created by the protest committee between the recruits and their senior officers by portraying the ex-RIC men as being akin to the unpopular corps of the Black and Tans.

3

THE OUTBREAK OF MUTINY

15 MAY

On the morning of 15 May 1922, the training of the Civic Guard came to an abrupt halt following the protest committee's decision to issue Staines with an ultimatum in response to the recent senior appointments within the force.[1] The ultimatum, signed by the representatives of seven of the companies of men, was issued by Daly and Sellars through the adjutant's office in the form of a letter 'demanding the immediate expulsion of five particular ex-RIC men, and threatening drastic action in case of non-compliance with the demand'.[2] The committee considered the promotion of the five listed men as a betrayal to the body of recruits who had served in the IRA, and they cited four reasons for their ultimatum. First, they objected to 'the high offices the five members held in the Civic Guard'. Second, they claimed that the five men had already exerted excessive influence over the commissioner. Third, the committee stated that the five men organised a recent increase in the recruitment of ex-RIC men to the Civic Guard. Fourth, the committee concluded that the RIC training methods employed by the men merely served to mould 'the new Irish police force … into a second edition of the Royal Irish Constabulary'.[3] The five members of the headquarters staff cited for expulsion were Deputy Commissioner Patrick Walsh, Private Secretary Jeremiah Maher and Superintendents Edmond Prendiville, James Brennan and Bernard O'Connor, despite the fact that each of these men appeared to have aided the IRA during the War of Independence.[4]

DEPUTY COMMISSIONER PATRICK WALSH

Born in Carrickaduff, County Monaghan, in 1871, Walsh joined the RIC in 1890. After eight years' service he was promoted to sergeant and in 1907 attained the rank of head constable. In 1911 Walsh was again promoted, to district inspector, and was serving in Letterkenny Barracks, County Donegal, when he received a personal invitation from Michael Collins to assist the organising committee, on the recommendation of a prominent Sinn Féin leader in Letterkenny, Dr Patrick McGinley. McGinley reported that during the War of Independence Walsh had prevented the Black and Tans from engaging in violent acts of retaliation and had personally hidden incriminating literature and shotgun cartridges in the midst of a police raid on McGinley's home.[5] In addition to his assistance with local Sinn Féin activists, Walsh was regarded as General Eoin O'Duffy's 'most valuable informant'.[6] On 15 February 1920, O'Duffy and Ernie O'Malley led the first IRA capture of an RIC barracks at Ballytrain, County Monaghan. The numerous exploits of O'Duffy during the War of Inde-

pendence prompted Collins to describe the County Monaghan leader as 'the best man by far in Ulster'.[7] Walsh was a
cousin of O'Duffy and briefed him when he returned from
official visits to Dublin Castle.

SUPERINTENDENT JEREMIAH MAHER

Jeremiah Maher was born in 1876 in County Meath. On
entering the RIC as a nineteen-year-old in 1895, Maher
served in numerous counties, including Clare, Meath, Carlow,
Waterford, Kilkenny and Mayo. During his service as a sergeant
in the RIC, Maher was transferred in December 1916 to the
county inspector's office in Naas, County Kildare. This position
allowed Maher to supply Collins with highly confidential
information.[8] Following his resignation from the force in July
1920, Maher became a member of the IRA in September of
that year, and was appointed intelligence officer in the 1st
and 4th Eastern Divisions of the IRA under the command
of Colonel-Commandant Seán Boylan of Dunboyne, County
Meath.[9] On examining the committee's ultimatum on 15
May, Maher was surprised to find it had wrongly claimed that
he had served in the RIC until the signing of the Anglo-Irish
Treaty in December 1921. Before the Treaty negotiations,
Maher had been elected to Kildare County Council and had
represented his local Sinn Féin branch as a delegate for the
party's annual Ard-Fheis.[10] Following a personal request from
Collins to join the organising committee, Maher accepted,
and over subsequent months Staines and Maher established
a strong working relationship. The depth of Maher's police

experience was appreciated by Staines, and at the earliest opportunity the commissioner appointed Maher as his private secretary following his admittance to the Civic Guard on 1 April 1922.

SUPERINTENDENT EDMOND PRENDIVILLE

Edmond Prendiville was born in County Kerry in 1871. He joined the RIC at the age of twenty-four and served in the counties of Monaghan, Limerick and Cork, and in the city of Belfast. Six years after joining the RIC, Prendiville was promoted to sergeant. He remained at this rank for the following eighteen years until he was demobilised from the force on 3 April 1922. The following day, he was enlisted into the Civic Guard. Prendiville claimed that he had approached a senior Sinn Féin member during the War of Independence about his intention to retire from the force and stated that 'he advised me not to on any account, that I was much more useful where I was'.[11] Before his demobilisation, Prendiville had been serving in Clonmel, County Tipperary, and was active in the RIC Representative Body. He was part of a delegation that travelled three times to London in 1921 to discuss future policing arrangements in Ireland with Sir Hamar Greenwood. During the course of the meetings, he came into 'constant touch' with senior Sinn Féin representatives at the Treaty negotiations, and was later asked to become a member of the organising committee.[12] On accepting a place on the committee, Prendiville was placed on the 'Training' sub-committee and offered a position in the Civic Guard: 'I didn't ask to get into the Civic Guard, I was simply invited in there and did my best.'[13]

SUPERINTENDENT JAMES BRENNAN

James Brennan was born in County Mayo in 1874. He joined the RIC at twenty-two years of age and served in the counties of Roscommon, Cork, Cavan and Galway before being transferred back to the RIC depot in April 1920. Details of Head Constable James Brennan's nationalist credentials remain unknown, but Michael Collins asked him to become a member of the organising committee. On attending the first meeting in the Gresham Hotel, Dublin, Brennan was placed on the 'Organisation' sub-committee under the chairmanship of District Inspector Kearney. Brennan continued to serve in the RIC until his demobilisation on 3 April 1922. He was appointed to the Civic Guard three days later.[14] According to his service file, he received an RIC pension of £236.13s.4d. per annum (equal to about £5,000 in the 2000s).

SUPERINTENDENT BERNARD O'CONNOR

Born in County Roscommon in 1870, Bernard O'Connor joined the RIC in January 1889 and served in the counties of Longford, Galway, Limerick, Waterford and Mayo. He rose through the ranks and was promoted to the post of district inspector on his transfer to Claremorris, County Mayo. O'Connor claimed that during the War of Independence his assistance to the IRA drew the attention of his superiors and:

on 7th June 1920 I ceased to work in the RIC at that time for some certain reasons that were never mentioned. I was transferred to Edenderry. In consequence of what we all know I was about putting in my resignation but I didn't get time because I was told to go … I was told to apply for my pension or I would be compulsorily retired.[15]

Unusually, the entry details in O'Connor's RIC service records regarding his departure from the force were left blank. Although O'Connor was not a member of the organising committee, he received one of the earliest appointments in the Civic Guard, and on 27 February was appointed as measuring and receiving officer. He later testified that Staines had little option but to recruit him as an officer in the Civic Guard because 'if it had to go further Mr Collins would appoint me'.[16]

Staines responded to the ultimatum to expel these men by requiring Commandant Ring to call for a General Parade to be held at 2 p.m. that day. Thirty minutes after the men had assembled on the parade grounds, Staines arrived and ordered Adjutant Haugh to call the men to attention. Staines read out the names of the latest appointments and later recalled that 'it was apparent at once that some secret agitation had been fomented and that what should have been a disciplined force was in the process of being converted into an unruly mob'.[17] The commissioner also claimed that the committee was unwittingly leading the recruits astray: 'It was at once apparent that some secret propaganda had been at work and that the unthinking men were being led away by some unscrupulous agency.'[18] During the address, Ring stood beside Staines and later testified that the commissioner then informed the men that he had just received an ultimatum:

> He spoke to them and told them that he could not take a demand and that they should send it in the form of a request. He called out the committee and asked them were they the signatories of it. They said yes, and that they meant to stand by what they said.[19]

Staines addressed the body of approximately 1,250 men and sought to clarify the contribution of the contentious ex-RIC men to the cause of Irish independence, insisting that 'they had done more work for Ireland than the men who now demanded their expulsion'.[20] Staines then called on each signatory of the ultimatum to stand in the centre of the square and to state their registration number.[21] He asked the assembled members of the committee if the matter was now closed and, if so, that they return to the lines of the parade. Instead of accepting the commissioner's attempted conclusion, the leaders of the committee defied Staines and refused to rejoin the lines of the parade. In response, Staines 'advised them to send in their resignations'.[22] The commissioner then spent a moment discussing the situation with Ring, and asked the body of men if they would stand by him or by the committee. The reaction of the men to Staines' question resulted in heckling and the breaking of ranks. The vast majority of the men moved towards the protest committee, leaving Staines in an excited state as he exclaimed that the men were little more than 'a pack of hooligans'.[23] 'Seeing that matters were at a crisis, and that the discipline of the Guard had been undermined', Staines dismissed the parade.[24]

During the retreat of the headquarters staff to their offices, the commissioner heard a section of the recruits shouting out, 'We'll stand by Paddy Brennan.' Staines perceived the cries of support for Brennan as a threat to his position as commissioner. He later insinuated that Brennan had been provoking hostility among the men towards himself in the previous weeks, and that the shouts of support for Brennan as an alternative commissioner were not surprising.[25] Ring remained defiantly before the men and identified Sergeant Rochford as the leading voice in support of the absent Brennan, whose failure to return from leave on the day of the mutiny had incensed Staines: 'Up to this time, the Assistant Commissioner had not returned, although his leave had expired the previous day, nor had he applied for any extension.'[26] Brennan later testified that he was visiting his sick mother in Meelick and had conceded to her request to stay the night, with the remoteness of the house making it impossible for him to seek an extension of his leave.[27] Brennan also denied accusations of inciting the men. According to him, the fact that men were shouting his name, 'does not mean at all that I was the leader of the revolt. That is no proof at all.'[28] Brennan tried to explain Rochford's exuberance by clarifying that he had been his superior officer in the IRA and that the shouts were probably made 'on the spur of the moment' as the men broke ranks: 'Rochford is an East-Clare [*sic*] man and a member of the East Clare Column. Certainly when fellows have been knocking round together in all kinds of queer places, they have a kind of attachment for one another.'[29]

Amid the chaos on the parade ground, Ring remained before the men and called for calm. He reminded them of his own IRA background and achievements. He then asked the dissident recruits whether they would stand by him: 'They all said they would stand by me – the committee and all.'

In a statement of the day's events issued on behalf of the recruits, the details largely match the commandant's version, with the exception of the claim by Ring that nearly all the men proclaimed their loyalty to him. Instead, the statement alleged that Ring used the occasion to proclaim his personal contribution to the attainment of national independence:

> His address was, for the most part, a paean of self-adulation, which stuck in the nostrils of the men of the Guard who had done 'their bit' and would not think about 'bluffing' about it. Mr Ring began by stating that his record was better than any other man in the Depot. He said he had been in jail, had been on hunger strike, that his house had been burned down and that he had fought against England more than anyone else. 'I am not a policeman or a Black and Tan,' he shouted, 'and will you stand by me?' Only a few from his native place stood behind him. The remainder of the men remained with the committee.[30]

Ring asked the men to reconsider the ultimatum and recalled that two men in particular, O'Meara and Healy, became highly agitated and began shouting and roaring their disapproval of ex-RIC men being appointed to senior positions. Ring reminded the men that as a former IRA column leader during the War of Independence, he had relied on the information he received from the police and 'certainly admired those police who gave me this information'.[31] Unmoved by the commandant's sentiments, O'Meara openly criticised Ring by claiming that 'you didn't fight straight if you took information from them', to which Ring responded 'if I didn't fight straight my bullets went straight'.[32]

Tensions continued to rise as the men stated their intention to 'throw those five men out of the Depot'. Ring replied that the removal of the five men would also require his physical removal from the depot and 'there is no man fit to put me out'.[33] Although Ring admitted that his response served only to raise tensions further, he succeeded in dismissing the parade and called on the committee members to remain behind to discuss matters further. Ring reiterated his earlier suggestion that they send in a request and promised the members that 'I would do my best'. The members of the protest committee then agreed to discuss the matter with the men. Ring advised the committee that Staines would have to leave the depot and report the events of the day to the government and implored the committee 'not to do anything drastic', at least until Staines returned. On agreeing that no action would take place and 'that everything would go on in the camp' as before, Ring and the committee concluded their discussion.[34] Later that evening, Ring informed the committee that Minister Duggan wished to meet two of their members in Government Buildings, Dublin, at 4 p.m. the next day.[35]

As the commissioner retreated to his office under the protection of his senior officers, around 100 dissident recruits set about raiding the armoury. On observing the large number of 'excited' recruits in his area, Barrack Master Mathias McCarthy 'thought it better not to interfere'.[36] McCarthy later testified that these recruits succeeded in taking 167 rifles and 243 revolvers from the original stockpile of 200 rifles and 1,000 revolvers.[37] Seán Liddy, aware that a proportion of the arms had already been dispersed among the dissident recruits, became concerned about the safety of Staines and the headquarters staff, and ordered 'a special armed guard as a precautionary measure to ensure the safety of the men who had locked themselves in'.[38]

16 MAY

On the morning of 16 May, Staines decided not to order normal daily parades and training. Instead, the commissioner sought to divide the large number of recruits in Kildare by ordering Ring to make the necessary arrangements for the transfer of No. 6 Company, the only company not to have a representative on the committee, to the nearby vacant barracks at Newbridge.[39] At ten o'clock in the morning, Ring went to the transport stores within the depot to ensure that

No. 6 Company was ready to board the trucks for Newbridge. However, on his arrival he was confronted by members of the protest committee, who were advising the men of No. 6 Company not to board the trucks. The committee described the transfer 'as an attempt to divide the Guard into small parts ... and a breach of the Agreement arrived at between Mr Ring and the committee'.[40] Ring informed those present that his orders were to take over Newbridge Barracks and said he was 'going to take it over if I had only five men'. He stated that any recruits willing to obey orders should get into trucks.[41] Following Ring's intercession, Staines travelled with the entire company of approximately 200 recruits and entered the recently evacuated British army barracks.[42] On his return, Staines claimed that his authority had been diminished by the protest committee who, he later testified, had assumed control of the depot and whose members were issuing the recruits with orders of their own: 'Seeing the situation was impossible, and that the men allowed themselves to be influenced by a number of their comrades who were not amenable to reason, I left the Depot and came to Dublin and reported the matter to the Provisional Government.'[43]

Before embarking on his journey, accompanied by Patrick Walsh, Staines completed two tasks. First, he took the precautionary step at 1.30 p.m. of requesting Superintendent John Joseph Byrne to seek immediate military assistance with the transfer of the Civic Guard armoury to the custody of the National Army.[44] Ironically, Byrne had been the 'organiser' of the first protest against the presence of ex-RIC men in the

RDS, but by this stage his loyalties seem to have changed. He was instructed by Staines to travel to the Curragh Camp and to request that Lieutenant General J. J. O'Connell dispatch the required military assistance.[45] Second, Staines wrote to the minister for home affairs, Éamonn Duggan, and offered his resignation 'with great regret, but in the circumstances which have arisen I can see no other honourable course open … I feel that I can no longer serve as commissioner of the Civic Guard, and … therefore ask to be relieved of my command at the earliest possible moment.'[46] Deputy Commissioner Walsh also tendered his resignation before they both journeyed to Government Buildings for the arranged meeting with Duggan, Collins and two representatives of the protest committee. On the instructions of Staines, Ring remained in his quarters and awaited further instructions.[47]

At 6 p.m. the meeting at Government Buildings began with Collins and Duggan requesting that the two committee representatives, Thomas Daly and Patrick Sellars, explain the reasons behind the signing and issuing of an ultimatum to Staines on behalf of the protest committee. Then they issued Daly and Sellars with a document outlining the government's proposals to conclude the dispute, which required the grievances of the men to be put in writing and an immediate return to the status quo. Once both requirements had been fulfilled, the government proposed to establish an enquiry into the dispute. Sellars recalled that they were asked to return to the depot, to consult with the other members of the committee and to forward their response in writing.[48] Following the departure of Daly and Sellars, Collins presumed that the committee would accept the government's terms for the return of Staines and his staff. Staines was ordered by Collins to return to the depot later in the evening and to reassert his authority as commissioner of the Civic Guard.

While Staines, Walsh, Sellars and Daly had been making their way to Dublin for their meeting with Collins and Duggan, Superintendent Byrne returned to Kildare Barracks with a truckload of soldiers from the Curragh. These men waited for forty-five minutes for the arrival of an armoured car, which was travelling from Beggar's Bush, Dublin, before taking any action.[49] As the military prepared to advance through the gates of the barracks, the remaining arsenal was dispersed among the dissident recruits under the command of one of the leading committee members, Guard John O'Meara. Ring recalled making his way to meet the truck as the recruits 'were running everywhere they could get cover. Rifles were pointing at me as I was passing down to the gate, not pointed towards the armoured car but on me, but it didn't frighten me.'[50] On his arrival at the gates of the barracks, Captain Corry, the officer in charge, who was already being briefed by Byrne, was met by both Ring and Superintendent Seán Liddy, TD. Corry asked Ring and Liddy, 'What is the trouble here?' Liddy asserted, 'I am a representative here,' at which Ring interjected, 'You are not, I am the commandant of the Camp', and informed Corry that the camp was in a state of mutiny and 'that the arms of the camp were being seized and all control taken out of my hands'.[51] Ring claimed that the committee had orchestrated the mutiny and were attempting to turn the barracks over to the 'Irregulars'.[52]

Such an accusation by the commandant was described by the dissident recruits as a treacherous untruth and they claimed that Ring was intent on inciting 'Dáil Troops to turn a machine-gun on the Camp of the Civic Guard'.[53] Liddy later testified that Ring had instructed Corry to carry out his orders, and that he wanted 'to see them blown to Hell out of here, the pack of hooligans'.[54] Corry turned to Liddy and gave him 'ten minutes from now to open the gate, otherwise I will force it open'. Liddy advised Corry to look 'in the direction of the avenue, from which three hundred rifles were trained on the gate'.[55]

After a further conversation with Corry, Liddy claimed that he telephoned the captain's superior officer in his capacity as a pro-Treaty TD, and convinced the military that the 'Irregulars' were not in control of the camp and that the dispute was an internal issue which need not end in bloodshed. Furthermore, Liddy reminded the military that Staines was not at the depot and that his presence was required for the orders to be executed. Liddy was later instructed by the superior officer to 'go and tell Captain Corry to report back to me immediately, to Beggar's Bush'.[56]

Recruit James Donohue considered the dissolution of the conflict between two newly formed institutions of the Provisional Government to be crucial, 'for had the discharge of a single firearm occurred, it might have altered the course of events, not only of that day and of the formation of a police force, but of the future politically'.[57]

Following the departure of the military, the remaining headquarters staff and the recruits withdrew to their quarters. At 9 p.m. Assistant Commissioner Brennan finally returned to the depot from his extended visit to County Clare. On entering the depot that evening, Brennan was met by Superintendent Bernard O'Connor, one of the five men listed in the committee's ultimatum for dismissal. He explained to Brennan that the headquarters staff had effectively been abandoned since Staines' earlier departure. He recalled telling Brennan that the deserted high-ranking officers felt themselves to be in a quandary, as they wished to follow Staines to Dublin but were refused permission to leave the depot by guards at the gate. O'Connor had tried to reason with the guards and told them that 'it was a nice thing to order men out of the depot and then when they wanted to get out, they wouldn't let them out'.[58] Brennan agreed that 'it was better for the men concerned to go out of the depot' and arranged immediately for their transportation to Kildare Railway Station. O'Connor later testified that Brennan was 'most agreeable' in providing a safe passage for the high-ranking officers.[59]

Following Collins' earlier order to return to the Kildare Barracks, Staines arrived at the gates at 10.30 p.m. The sentries refused to admit the commissioner but agreed to dispatch a messenger to alert Brennan that Staines was outside. Brennan later stated that he had just made his way to the officers' mess, where Liddy, Haugh and Lynch had begun to update him about the serious developments that had taken place at the camp: 'I got some grub, I was in the officers' mess, and a messenger came into me and said Mr Staines was outside, and the sentries did not want to let him in. "Is he to be let in?" he asked. I said "Yes, he is to be let in. He is the commissioner."'[60] In the interim, Thomas Daly and other members of the protest committee had arrived at the gates and refused to allow the commissioner entry 'in the interests of peace'. The committee said that Staines would not be allowed in as he had allegedly endangered the lives of the Civic Guards by calling on the military to seize the camp, and he had also claimed that the barracks was being held by the 'Irregulars'.[61] Despite his efforts to negotiate, Staines 'was compelled again to return to Dublin'.[62] Brennan later asserted that he had only become aware the next morning that the committee had overridden his order and 'had refused to let Mr Staines in'.[63]

17 MAY

The committee initiated plans for the regularisation of the camp on the morning of 17 May. Routine Orders were drawn up for the day and included a list of appointments to replace Staines and his exiled staff. Assistant Commissioner Brennan was listed as commissioner; Superintendent P. J. Haugh was appointed as assistant commissioner; Superintendent Lynch was appointed as commandant; and Seán Liddy was selected as the adjutant.[64] In an attempt to dispel any apprehension in relation to the allegiance of the Civic Guard and its submission to the lawful authority of the Provisional Government, a

Declaration of Loyalty was inserted as a paragraph in the Routine Orders: 'We declare our loyalty, and the loyalty of the members of the Civic Guard, to the Provisional Government and Dáil Éireann. – By Order of the Committee.' Brennan later claimed that he was never actually consulted nor accepted the position of commissioner and 'after a few days' he instructed Lynch, Liddy and Haugh to carry out their normal duties as previously assigned by Staines.[65] However, all four senior officers continued to engage with the committee for the duration of the mutiny.

18 MAY

Following their perusal of the document issued on 16 May by the Provisional Government to Daly and Sellars, the committee requested Brennan on 18 May to take their written response to Duggan. Almost the entire communication consisted of, 'Your reply unsatisfactory and cannot be entertained by committee.'[66] Brennan considered the response as 'rather comical. I told them afterwards … I was made the messenger who brought that up. I was coming up to a Dáil meeting. I had a further confab with Mr Duggan and Mr Collins … They said the committee would have to withdraw the demand and if they liked, put it in a request, and that there would be an Enquiry held.'[67] Liddy and Staines were also present at the meeting, and Brennan later maintained that 'I asked Mr Staines that day about ten times to come back to the Depot as commissioner, and that I would do my utmost, even if I had to risk my life, to get the men back to normal. He said "no", that he had resigned and would have nothing more to do with the Civic Guard. Mr Liddy can prove that, so can Mr Duggan and Mr Collins, if they remember it.'[68] Before the conclusion of the meeting in which 'cross' words were directed towards the assistant commissioner, Brennan claimed, 'I wound up by taking it on myself to go back to the Camp and try and fix up matters.'[69]

On Brennan's return from the meeting, he briefed the committee and, according to Sellars, the lack of progress prompted some men to resign their positions as members of the committee.[70] Such a vacuum allowed Daly to surround himself with men he knew were secretly loyal to the 'Irregular forces'. On the same day, Commandant Ring was in his quarters when a clerk of his office, Sergeant Keenan, entered and showed him a file issued by the committee which had correspondence with the signature of former organising committee member, Martin Lynch, as commandant of the depot.[71] Keenan, a retired member of the RIC, also showed Ring written confirmation that his services as a clerk were no longer required by the committee in the office of the commandant and he asked Ring for permission to remain in his quarters, fearing for his personal safety.[72] Ring was annoyed that the committee had appointed his replacement as commandant despite his presence in the depot. On hearing of these developments, Ring armed himself with his own handgun and prepared for a showdown with the committee.

A few hours later, men seeking refuge – recruits who had previously served in an IRA active service unit under Ring's command – entered Ring's quarters. These Mayo recruits felt compelled to go to Ring's quarters as they had been identified by the committee as his supporters and had been refused food.[73] The Mayo men were soon followed by Sergeant Frank Murray of the Transport Section, who had been placed under arrest by the committee and detained in a hut following his refusal to take orders from anyone but Commandant Ring.[74] During his captivity, Murray was allowed to write a note addressed to Acting Commandant Lynch. Murray informed Lynch that if he was not released, he would go on hunger strike. Lynch responded by ordering his immediate removal from the depot. Murray asked for permission to gather his clothes before departing, but on making his way towards his room, he ran to Ring's quarters, pursued by two recruits bearing arms. On hearing the commotion, Ring opened his door, drew his revolver and ordered the two recruits to back away from his quarters.

19 MAY

On the following day John O'Meara and other committee members made their way to Ring's quarters. Ring appeared at the door and was informed by O'Meara that he wanted to claim a watch belonging to McDowell, a driver in the Transport Section. According to O'Meara, the watch had previously been in the possession of Murray. O'Meara warned Ring not to interfere or 'I will take you out of it'.

'If that's your challenge, I will take your challenge to take me out.'[75]

On consulting with Murray, Ring was satisfied with his explanation that he had returned McDowell's watch to one of the guards when he had been detained in the hut. Following further verbal exchanges of threats, O'Meara and his comrades reluctantly withdrew, and soon afterwards the committee ordered two more men from the Transport Section, McDonagh and Byrne, to leave the depot. Instead, they made their way to Ring's quarters, where all the men had their own personal firearms.[76] The committee responded to the latest defections by placing guards at the front of the quarters, which prevented food supplies from reaching Ring and the men. Likewise, communication with Commissioner Staines was cut off because they were unable to access the telephones. In an effort to update Staines about their predicament, Ring employed diversionary tactics by conversing with two committee members from an upstairs window while two of the besieged, Guard Jim Staines and Superintendent John Keane, made their way out of the back of the house, but they were seen by two sentries, who gave chase. Guard Staines 'held the two sentries up' and Keane got through the wire and over the wall of the depot. On making his way back to Dublin, Keane arranged a meeting with Commissioner Staines at the Clarence Hotel that evening and was surprised 'when he told me that arrangements had been made with the assistant commissioner to allow Commandant Ring to leave the depot with these men and that they were to be given transport to bring them to Dublin'.[77]

SEARCH FOR A COMPROMISE

On the agreed evacuation of Ring and his comrades from Kildare Barracks, Daly and Sellars used the occasion to write a short letter to Duggan on behalf of the protest committee. Both men informed the minister that the committee wished to withdraw their earlier 'demand' of 15 May for the expulsion of ex-RIC men from the Civic Guard and asked for it to be treated instead as an 'informal' request. However, they also insisted that the government provide a 'guarantee' to the committee that their request would be met and stated that, on the removal of the five listed ex-RIC members, the committee would be 'prepared to meet you in every possible way'.[78] The letter was later described by Walsh as tantamount 'to saying that I won't shoot you in the heart, but I will blow your brains out'.[79]

On meeting Duggan and Collins to discuss the committee's latest proposal, Brennan recalled the reactions of the senior politicians: 'Mr Duggan kicked up a row about the guarantee. Mr Collins said they mean all right, but they do not want to give up the sponge altogether, to give an absolute surrender.'[80] Following government consideration of the committee's document, Brennan and Liddy were summoned to attend a departmental meeting at Government Buildings on 22 May with Collins and Duggan. During the meeting, Brennan recalled being surprised by Staines' accusation 'on me in the presence of Mr Collins and Mr Duggan that I engineered that row'. Brennan felt betrayed by Staines and was placed in an 'extraordinary situation' as he felt obliged to convince Collins that the only reason for his enduring presence in the depot was to ensure order among the recruits. Brennan also assured Collins of his full loyalty to the Provisional Government.[81]

Liddy's recollection focused on the aggressive manner of Collins: 'Liddy, what is your explanation for your conduct down in Kildare?' Liddy responded by reminding Collins that over 1,000 men of IRA origin stationed in Kildare and Newbridge Barracks 'strongly object to disbanded RIC men being promoted to commissioned rank'.

Collins interrupted Liddy and declared, 'Liddy, you know as well as I do what the country owes these men.'

According to Liddy, Collins then requested the adjutant of the mutineers to proffer his own resolution to the impasse, to which Liddy retorted, 'I should hand them their pieces of silver and call it a deal.'

Before the furious Collins stamped out of the room, he banged the table and shouted, 'By ____, if I smashed [sic] the country by it, these men will remain in the Force.'[82]

At this point, Duggan was left with no alternative but to close the meeting. On leaving Government Buildings, Brennan confided in Liddy that he feared they would be detained in Mountjoy Jail. Liddy reminded him that they still retained a 'trump card', as Collins relied on both of them to maintain the stability of the new state with the inevitability of civil war looming: 'No, sir, we are both TDs, they need our support.' However, on returning to Kildare, their confidence began to ebb as they shared a 'feeling that the abrupt ending of the meeting meant some form of Government action would swiftly follow'.[83]

Two pieces of correspondence were issued on the same evening. In the first letter, Daly and Sellars wrote to Duggan and informed the minister that:

> ... we hereby hand over the Headquarters and Depot of the Civic Guard to the Senior Officer here at present: Co. Commdt P. Brennan. We formally withdraw the word demand on original document and respectfully request the Minister for Home Affairs to have the grievances of the men inquired into as soon as possible. In future we shall have our lawful grievances put forward in the proper manner.[84]

The second piece of correspondence, dispatched to the Department of Home Affairs, included a copy of a four-point circular issued by Brennan to all men in Kildare Barracks. The circular began with Brennan's confirmation that the committee 'has withdrawn the *Demand* relative to certain ex-RIC put forward on the 15th May, 1922'. In his second point, Brennan personally accepted the transfer of full control of headquarters and the training depot, 'with instructions to consult with the Government and arrange a return to normal conditions'. In his third point, Brennan reminded the recruits that they must maintain 'unflinching obedience pledged to our country in the Declaration of Loyalty of 17th May, 1922'. In his concluding point, the assistant commissioner confirmed that the recent acts of indiscipline carried out by the recruits 'were born of a great and pure instinct ... in moments of tactless handling. You are back to normal. Remain at your posts, assured that the

Government to which you have now confidently entrusted your fortunes, will not prove *little*.'[85]

A PERSONAL VISIT BY COLLINS

On receiving the conciliatory correspondence from Kildare Barracks, Collins decided to visit the depot and address the men on Friday 26 May. Following his arrival, Collins held a short meeting with Brennan and asked him whether he should meet the protest committee or address the men at a General Parade. Brennan advised, 'See the Committee first, and see the men afterwards. Because if you do not try and placate them first you may be creating trouble. One or two men can kick up a dust anywhere.'[86]

On meeting the committee, discussions broke down on two occasions. Brennan described himself as a mediator and later quipped that the verbal exchanges were comparable to that experienced by Collins during the course of the Anglo-Irish Treaty negotiations: 'It was like Lloyd George and himself a third time. I brought them together and they agreed to return to status quo and have an enquiry.'[87] Finally, a compromise was reached between Collins and the committee allowing, as Brennan said, for the establishment of an enquiry and the return of the depot 'to status quo, that is that all men [Staines and his staff] would return the next morning if they wished'.[88]

Collins then addressed the body of men and informed them that the recent serious breaches of discipline had necessitated his arrival at Kildare in his capacity as leader of the government. He expressed particular 'disappointment' with the occurrences in the depot, as the government had sought to recruit a body of men that could be relied upon to assist the smooth establishment of the Civic Guard. Collins openly criticised the dissident recruits for their rash methods in seeking to air their grievances, but also explained that if they submitted any complaint, it 'would have had sympathetic consideration if it had been submitted in the ordinary way through the proper channels'. He reminded the men that 'a higher standard of discipline is required in a police force than in any other body', as it is the responsibility of the police 'to enforce discipline on others'.[89] Collins concluded his address by encouraging all recruits to maintain high standards of discipline and training, as they would have the opportunity to differentiate themselves from the RIC by serving the people of Ireland rather than a foreign country:

> When you go out amongst the people and take up your duties, your conduct will contrast favourably in every way with that of the force whose place you are filling. You will have one great advantage over any previous regular police force in Ireland and that is that you will start off with the good will of the people ... You will be their guardians, not their oppressors; your authority will be derived from the people, not from their enemies.[90]

'COLD WAR'

The impetus for Collins' visit to Kildare was not only the committee's withdrawal of its 'demand', but also the increasing threat posed by the Executive Forces to national security. Since

14 April, Rory O'Connor and his comrades had continued to hold the Four Courts without government interference, as any attempt to repossess the buildings would inevitably have instigated civil war. Collins' reluctance to take military action against the occupiers of the Four Courts was a growing source of frustration to the British government. As political pressure was applied from London and the shadow of civil war loomed, Collins was eager to conclude the mutiny and use the resources of the Civic Guard. The apparent resolution of the mutiny on 26 May eased Collins' anxieties that disgruntled Civic Guard recruits might transfer their loyalty from the Provisional Government to the Executive Force as 'the force of 1,500 trained and partially armed men in the Kildare Barracks would be an important factor in the Civil War and they would certainly be a welcome addition to one side or the other'.[91]

Although Collins and the committee resolved the dispute, Sellars was frustrated by the Provisional Government's lack of progress in arranging the formal return of the headquarters staff to Kildare Barracks: 'nobody turned up, and things dragged on … There was no returning of men or anything else, although the Depot was quite agreeable at the same time that the men would go back.'[92] As the dissident recruits awaited the return of Staines and his staff, a sense of distrust prevailed in the depot. Lynch sought to ensure the smooth return of the headquarters staff by issuing an order to the men for the return of arms to the armoury. However, he estimated that even after collecting over 110 rifles and 300 revolvers, the majority of the arms were still held by the men.[93]

Whether Collins was fully reassured about the loyalty of the recruits on his return from Kildare Barracks is questionable. Collins convinced Staines to remain as commissioner and, with the assistance of his staff, the ousted commissioner recruited an alternative police force in Dublin. Because of the difficulty of acquiring a suitable training depot, the new force was obliged to divide itself and move from its original centre at the Ormond Hotel to such venues as Little Denmark Street and Clonskeagh Castle in South County Dublin. Within months of the creation of the infant state, an extraordinary situation had developed: 'The new Civic Guard was divided into two rival groups, each with the full paraphernalia of a headquarters, a training centre and a recruitment office, one situated in Kildare under virtual siege by the government which created it, the other moving around Dublin City, taking accommodation wherever it might for a week or two at a time.'[94] The sudden acquisition of a warehouse by Staines and his latest batch of recruits under the cover of night on 22 May, drew the unwanted attention of national newspapers as the Provisional Government desperately attempted to keep the mutiny out of the public domain. Journalists were anxious to ascertain the reasons for the selection of premises far removed from the official commissioner's office in Kildare Barracks:

New Premises For Civic Guard: Why the furniture department of the Henry Street Warehouse Company in Little Denmark Street, Dublin, was taken possession of on Monday night by unarmed men is explained in an official announcement which was made yesterday by Commandant Staines, Commissioner of the Civic Guard. In his official capacity, Mr Staines stated that the premises have been for some time the property of the Provisional Government, and that no force was either used or was necessary in taking possession of them. The men who went into possession were recruits of the Civic Guard, and it is intended to use the upper portion of the premises for enrolling candidates for that organisation.[95]

According to Liddy, the situation became even more chaotic as a number of recruits who had joined Staines' new Civic Guard force in Dublin defected on learning of the mutiny and travelled to Kildare Barracks, where they joined their comrades. The influx of such recruits over a two-week period necessitated the transfer of additional companies of men to Newbridge Barracks. In a jubilant tone, the acting adjutant claimed, 'we had now, between Kildare and Newbridge, over two thousand men' in a state of recalcitrance.[96] Though Liddy and his mutineers celebrated their moral victory, they had been without pay since early May and accused the Provisional Government of conducting 'a cold war'.[97] However, without completed pay-shects, Staines was able to rebuff this allegation.

The establishment of a rival force by the Provisional Government provoked Brennan to place a Civic Guard recruitment notice in the national newspapers. Brennan took advantage of the government's wish to maintain a shroud of secrecy about earlier embarrassing events in the depot and inserted a claim that he alone possessed the authority to recruit for the

Civic Guard. Potential applicants were informed 'that they must not present themselves at the Training Camp, Kildare, until they have received calling-up notices from the assistant commissioner, who has sole charge of recruiting'.[98]

The protest committee became increasingly impatient that the promised enquiry into the dispute had yet to be established, and were aggrieved that Staines was attempting to train a new police force in Dublin. On 7 June Daly and Sellars travelled to Dublin 'to remind the Chairman of the Provisional Government that he had not fulfilled his agreement of May 26th'.[99] Collins was unavailable and requested that the men return to Dublin the following day for a scheduled meeting with Staines and himself. At the meeting, Daly and Sellars requested an immediate establishment of the promised enquiry and the payment of the men. Staines agreed that the payment would be arranged, on condition that a complete stocktake of the barracks was permitted.[100] Sellars later recalled that it was agreed that Deputy Commissioner Walsh would lead the delegation of the five men originally listed by the committee for expulsion into the barracks the following morning to conduct a full stocktake, and that Staines would accompany them.[101] It was also agreed that, on concluding the stocktake, the entire headquarters staff would be permitted to return to their quarters and normal duties the following day.[102]

9 JUNE

When Staines and an entourage of eleven men arrived at the gates of the barracks, according to the commissioner they were 'refused admittance without a pass, until a Guard came forward who stated he knew me'.[103] Staines was incensed that the guards at the gate had not been informed by Brennan of the agreed arrangements for their return to the depot and demanded Brennan's immediate presence at the gates. However, Staines was informed that Brennan had left the depot 'on a journey to the South. He had no permission to do so, and clearly went to avoid being present.'[104]

Brennan later testified that Liddy and himself had left to attend an anniversary mass in memory of their former comrades of East Clare, and accepted that their journey had not received official authorisation.[105] In contrast to Brennan's statement about his whereabouts, Liddy later testified that he was not in Kildare Barracks at the time of Staines' return because earlier in the week he had moved to and remained in Newbridge Barracks.[106]

As Staines waited outside the gates, the three most prominent members of the committee, Daly, Sellars and Sergeant Seán O'Brien, approached the gates. According to Staines, they 'took full control' and insisted that he had broken the terms of agreement as he had returned to the depot with a larger number of his staff than had been agreed previously with Collins. Staines insisted that 'my instructions from Mr Collins, who was responsible for the agreement, were that I was to come down to Kildare to take stock, and that I was to bring as many members of the Civic Guard, officers and men as I thought fit'. Staines argued that there was no possible way that he would agree to lead only the five men originally objected to by the committee back into a depot of unpaid dissident recruits.[107] Instead, Staines insisted that Collins had set no limit to the number of men that could accompany him back into Kildare Barracks and distinctly remembered Collins saying, 'Bring down as many as you need, we will leave it to yourself.' As the dispute continued at the gates, Sellars claimed that Staines told the three committee members that he was now assuming full control 'and that the committee should cease to exist'.[108] While refusing Staines admittance, the committee told him that he should instead return to Dublin and arrange for the immediate payment of the men as they were as much entitled to their monthly salary as the latest batches of recruits being trained in Dublin. The commissioner replied that he knew all about the men in Dublin and nothing about the men in Kildare.[109] Before his return to Dublin, Staines observed that the committee held full control of the depot and that 'the situation was far from normal as claimed, even the meaning of discipline was lost', which was in stark contrast to the earlier written statements sent by Brennan to Duggan on 22 May, which claimed that he had assumed control of affairs in the depot.[110] Staines concluded that Brennan's correspondence was 'the merest nonsense, and calculated to deceive the authorities. The committee were still in full control, and the officers were mere ciphers.'[111]

Unaware that Staines and his headquarters staff had yet again returned to Dublin, two of his staff, Superintendent Byrne and Sergeant McAvinia, had travelled from Clonskeagh Castle to join the commissioner. They presented themselves at 7.30 p.m. before Guard Costello at the gates of Kildare Barracks. While Costello initially insisted that any person seeking entry required a pass, he subsequently agreed to allow Byrne and McAvinia to enter the depot. On seeking their comrades in various quarters, McAvinia asked a passing guard whether he had seen the commissioner. The response was that he had been seen earlier but had since returned to Dublin.[112] As Byrne and McAvinia continued to search for any of their party, they met Sergeant Patrick Doyle, who requested that the men show their passes. As they did not possess passes, Doyle ordered them to leave the depot. As both men turned towards the gates, Adjutant Haugh emerged from the receiving office and, on recognising both men, he returned to the office and alerted dissident recruits in the vicinity. Byrne later testified that by the time they reached the gates, thirty guards were pursuing them while hissing and chanting 'Black and Tans'.[113] As Byrne and McAvinia decided to make their way towards Kildare town, the crowd following them increased to an estimated 100 men. Sporadic shouts of 'Byrne, you have not your armoured car now' were heard by both men and referred specifically to Byrne's request on 16 May for an armoured car to seize the armoury of the depot.

The depth of antipathy directed towards Byrne was not only attributable to his direct involvement with the military, but also a result of the men's sense of betrayal by their former IRA colleague. As a founding member of the original protest committee in the RDS, which had demanded the immediate expulsion of Kearney, Byrne had attained trust and respect among the recruits. Following his subsequent promotion to Superintendent, Byrne's display of loyalty to Staines on the day of the mutiny had drawn the ire of the crowd who now followed him around the streets of Kildare. McAvinia had previously served in the RIC, which he had joined in 1914 but resigned from in April 1918 because of his nationalist sympathies.[114] He later assisted Staines as a member of the Republican Police and was invited to apply to join the Civic Guard.[115] In Kildare, he was appointed by Staines as mess caterer and accompanied the commissioner in the transfer of No. 6 Company to Newbridge despite the objections of the committee.[116] His loyalty to Staines and history with the RIC were enough to condemn him in the eyes of the dissident recruits, despite his later involvement with the republicans.

Both men considered their options. Byrne suggested entering the Railway Hotel to telephone the commissioner for instructions, but McAvinia proposed making their way to the railway station as he thought a train would be leaving at that time. On entering the station, Byrne estimated that the crowd had reached hundreds of people, because many local people had joined the dissident recruits on hearing the chants of 'Black and Tans'. Within a few minutes, Byrne was shocked to see that 'the road was chock full'. Much to their dismay, the station master informed Byrne and McAvinia that the next train stopping at the station would not be until 2.30 a.m. As the crowd began to close in around them, Byrne identified two recruits, Healy and Burke, as the main ringleaders who were inciting the crowd to follow the men.

As Byrne and McAvinia made their way towards the nearby Railway Hotel, they heard the crowd singing 'The Bold Black and Tans'. On entering the hotel, Mr Connolly, the proprietor of the premises, refused to allow Byrne to use the telephone. McAvinia recalled the manager speaking in an excited manner as he informed Byrne that 'some members of the crowd said they would burn the house if he didn't put us outside'.[117] Both men went back onto the streets of Kildare town and Byrne noticed Burke at his shoulder and heard an order for men to 'go back to the Barracks and get rifles'.[118] Burke then attempted to take Byrne's handgun and shouted at him, 'Here Byrne, I have something to say to you', when suddenly Sergeant McNamara, a former IRA battalion vice-commandant, drew his Colt .45 handgun and Byrne responded in kind. McAvinia reacted by drawing his handgun and turning towards the crowd.[119]

Following a short stand-off, McNamara shouted at the men, 'Close in, fellows, don't be afraid.' Byrne and McAvinia ran, and were fired on by McNamara: 'The bullet passed between myself and McAvinia. I heard the singing and the humming of the bullet passing between us. At the same time, people started throwing stones. I was hit three or four times in the shoulder and neck with stones.'[120] Byrne asserted that he had been 'on very good terms' with Sergeant McNamara before he requested military assistance to disarm the Civic Guards in the depot, and the reason he did not stand his ground was 'because there were a number of civilians around the Market Square at the time, and if I returned McNamara's fire somebody who was not belonging to the mob, or who was not with me, would probably have been hit. That's the only reason I didn't return fire'.[121]

McNamara later testified that he only drew the revolver when Byrne and McAvinia drew their revolvers on the crowd. According to him, the large number of people gathered around both men were 'getting more hostile'.[122] He claimed that he merely drew his revolver in consideration of the safety of the crowd and the two fleeing men: 'Then I drew my revolver and got right out to the front of him [Byrne]. He was not going to fire on the crowd as long as I was there ... The crowd got very excited and I saw that if they got him they would pull him to pieces. He ran and the crowd ran after him. I fired a shot up in the air to keep back the crowd.'[123] McNamara took exception to the allegation that he fired at the men, especially as he considered himself adept in the use of firearms and possessed the necessary expertise to hit the men if he so wished: 'I know as much about a revolver as Superintendent Byrne or Sergeant McAvinia. He may have had a revolver longer than me but he got it soft. I had to fight for it and it was from one of his dead comrades I got it.'[124]

As both men scurried through the streets, they saw the open front door of a private house and ran upstairs where they took refuge in a bedroom. On placing three American-style suitcases against the door, the men looked out the window and saw the occupants of the house quickly leaving and men with rifles took up positions outside the front of the house. Byrne and McAvinia quickly left the house by the back door, in heavy rain. Having run down a lane, they pleaded with an old man to allow them to take shelter in his cabin. As they crouched down in his home, Byrne recalled that:

> four or five patrols of men passed, and they carried rifles and canvas bandoliers, with .303 ammunition in them. They asked questions from some people around the place. I could hear them asking the woman who was staying in the cottage next door, as to where the men had gone. A woman told them we had gone away down the fields. They didn't search the house in which we were, but they searched several other houses around the place.[125]

Byrne anticipated that the recruits would have to return to the barracks by 10 p.m., and advised McAvinia that they should wait a little longer before making their way to the nearby village of Rathangan, from where they intended boarding a train back to Dublin the next day. However, on leaving the cabin at 10.20 p.m., they had only walked fifty yards before observing lines of men posted along their route, so abandoned their initial plan and travelled across fields towards Fr Brady's house at the nearby Carmelite church of White Abbey. After waiting for a patrol of men with rifles to pass the church, both men climbed over the wall and explained their predicament to Fr Brady, who agreed to allow them to stay the night. At 11 p.m. Fr Brady was confronted outside the grounds by a patrol composed of Civic Guards and locals from Kildare village. On his return to the house, Fr Brady informed both men that he had remonstrated with the patrol and they had eventually agreed to leave the area. The following day, Byrne and McAvinia finally made their way back to Dublin on the 12.30 p.m. train.[126]

THE HIDDEN AGENDA

In the midst of the mutiny, Commissioner Staines decided to try to retain his parliamentary seat in the general election of 16 June 1922. Three days before the election, news reached him that handbills were being stored in Kildare Barracks 'containing baseless statements intended to injuriously affect my candidature as TD'.[127] In the early hours of 15 June, recruits from Kildare Barracks arrived in Dublin to post handbills around the constituency of Dublin North West. Despite this attempted sabotage of his electoral hopes, Staines was re-elected. Similarly, Brennan and Liddy retained their Dáil Éireann seats in Clare.

Under the leadership of Michael Collins, the pro-Treaty faction of Sinn Féin enjoyed a decisive electoral triumph. However, their success served only to prompt the anti-Treaty faction into taking immediate and detrimental action against the Civic Guard. On the night of Saturday 17 June, Thomas Daly and his anti-Treaty faction finally emerged from within the camp at Kildare. At 11 p.m. Daly and his fellow committee member, Sergeant Seán O'Brien, went to the armoury and signed out 'a number of rifles and ammunition and revolvers'.[128] They then proceeded to the transport yard and ordered three tenders and one Ford car.

As Daly and O'Brien awaited their transport, Sergeant

Doyle, the acting orderly officer, asked why they needed transport at that late time of night and was told that they had received a phone call requesting the immediate transport of Civic Guards from the temporary training centre in Little Denmark Street to the Kildare Barracks.[129] Daly claimed that the men in Dublin wished to abandon Staines' new force and join their comrades in Kildare. While such a request 'had happened before on numerous occasions', Doyle was concerned about the late hour and asked Daly to inform Acting Commandant Lynch of his request for transport before their departure.[130] Daly went to Lynch's quarters and told him that he had already received the required authorisation from Brennan. Lynch did not believe Daly and decided to accompany him to the yard to consult with the officer in charge of transport. Lynch recalled that the three tenders and a Ford car had already 'been ordered before they approached me at all, and as a matter of fact, the men were getting their own arms from the armoury. I met the man in charge of the Transport, Delahunty. He seemed to have a suspicion about the cars going out at that hour.'[131] Lynch insisted that he would accompany the party on their journey to Dublin and called on Adjutant Haugh and Delahunty and six other guards to join him. Doyle remained at the depot and took the precaution of issuing each vehicle with a password for their return. Daly left in the Ford car thirty minutes ahead of the three tenders. Lynch led the first tender of the convoy, with O'Brien and Haugh following.

As the convoy made its way through the nearby Curragh,

Lynch stopped before 'a glaring light' and found the convoy confronted by an armoured car and three trucks packed with 'Irregular' soldiers who had been transported from the occupied Four Courts. Daly drove up to Lynch and told him they were surrounded on all sides and pointed to a nearby cottage, where the officers in charge of the 'Irregulars' were awaiting his arrival. On approaching the cottage, Lynch, Haugh and O'Brien were met by General Rory O'Connor, Major-General Ernie O'Malley and Commandant-General Tom Barry: 'We were asked to turn over. We were told that they had declared war on England, that they did not want to be fighting with Irishmen, and all that sort of thing and would we come along. I said, "No." They said, "Surely, O'Brien, you will fight anyhow?" O'Brien said "I do not mind having a fight any time."'[132] O'Connor made a final attempt to persuade Lynch that he and all the Civic Guards should assist the 'Irregulars' in their plan to overthrow the Provisional Government, and promised Lynch that they would pay the Civic Guards the money outstanding to them.[133] O'Connor also requested an opportunity to address the recruits to explain their intentions and provide members of the Civic Guard with an opportunity to join the Executive Forces.

On refusing to consider O'Connor's invitation, Lynch and Haugh were 'politely asked' to hand over their revolvers and told to march in the same company as fifteen Free State soldiers who had earlier been taken prisoner on the streets of Newbridge by O'Connor as a precautionary measure. Haugh recalled that as they walked towards the nearby cottage, 'I objected to being marched with them as an officer and I was told to fall back in the rear. I was put into a house with them. There was no distinction made between officers and men … The majority of these soldiers were under the influence of drink and I do not think they knew really what happened.'[134] Despite the encircling of the tenders by the 'Irregulars', Guards Delahunty and O'Dea managed to evade capture and 'Delahunty had put two cars out of action and they [Executive Forces] had to tow these two cars to Dublin.'[135] While attempting to return to barracks to raise the alarm, Delahunty and O'Dea lost their way in the Curragh and failed to reach the depot until 4 a.m.

In a quest for guns and ammunition for the anticipated civil war, the convoy of trucks and the armoured car was able to make its way back into Kildare Barracks, as Daly was able to proffer the password on request at the gates.[136] On arriving outside the armoury, three men approached the door of the building, which was under the supervision of Guard Michael Fallon. Fallon recalled three members of the committee making their way into the building at about 1.30 a.m. He recognised the men as Daly, O'Brien and Guard E. J. Ryan, and allowed them to enter. O'Brien held the door open for the entry of 'Irregular' soldiers, who rushed into the armoury and held up Fallon and the other guards. While Daly and his men set about collecting the remaining 88 rifles, 270 Colt .34s, 383 Colt .38s and five boxes of ammunition, Sergeant Patrick Doyle, the orderly officer, walked over to the armoury and questioned Ryan as to the whereabouts of Lynch and Haugh.[137] He was surprised to observe Civic Guards being accompanied by strangers coming out of the armoury with rifles:

> I saw Seán O'Brien coming down with an arm full of rifles. I said 'Where in the hell are those fellows going to?' He said 'Mind yourself now, we have turned over to the Executive Forces and we are declaring war on England on Monday' … Then he held me up. I had a revolver on me and he took it from me.[138]

Doyle, a native of County Longford and a veteran of the 1916 Rising, was approached by Tom Barry, 'the famous South West Cork Column commander', who was described by Assistant Commissioner Brennan as 'a great friend' of Daly's.[139] Barry shook Doyle's hand and misinformed him that the Civic Guards in the missing tenders were on their way to the Four Courts to assist the anti-Treaty military campaign and that Doyle should consider doing the same. Following their refusal to join the Executive Forces, the Civic Guards in the armoury were held as prisoners by O'Brien until 3.30 a.m. On his release, Doyle immediately alerted Brennan and told him of his fear that Lynch and Haugh had been taken prisoner: 'Mr Brennan advised me to do nothing until morning. "Well," he said, "you cannot go out now anyhow and you cannot serve any good purpose by going out." I remained up for the rest of the night.'[140]

As the 'Irregular' soldiers made their way from Kildare Barracks to the Four Courts, they stopped at the cottage in the Curragh to release the Civic Guard prisoners. The soldiers instructed the guards to remain in the cottage for another hour and told them they would be shot if they left before that time. Fifteen minutes after the 'Irregulars' had left, Lynch and the men made their way on foot back to the Kildare Barracks.[141] Liddy recalled that the following morning seven of the recruits at Newbridge Barracks and about 'a dozen others' at Kildare Barracks tendered their resignation in order to support the 'Irregulars'.[142] However, Liddy failed to mention that, at this time, five members of the committee had switched their allegiance to the 'Irregulars'.[143] The prominent defectors were Thomas Daly, Seán O'Brien, E. J. Ryan, Malachy Collison and John Doyle. On considering the events of the night, Brennan later remarked that the senior officers of the Executive Forces, O'Connor, Barry and O'Malley, had obviously been informed by Daly that they could 'take it for granted that they could come down and walk into the depot' and 'not merely take the arms and the ammunition, but the actual men'.[144]

The unexpected armoury raid of Ireland's first national police force by the enemies of the Provisional Government placed both the recruits and the authorities in an embarrassing situation. It was obvious to the men of the Civic Guard that their grievances had been manipulated effectively by a significant cohort of the committee to sabotage the establishment of the Civic Guard and to seize their armoury for use against the new state.

TRAGEDY IN NEWBRIDGE

Less than forty-eight hours after the raid, the first tragedy in the brief history of the Civic Guard occurred. On the night of 20 June, a group of five Civic Guards were out of barracks. After leaving a local public house in Newbridge town at around midnight, one of the men, Michael McKenna of Mohill, County Leitrim, accidentally shot and killed his cousin and neighbour, Farrell Leddy.[145] McKenna also shot another recruit in the head, but not fatally. According to an official statement made by McKenna, they were nearing the gates of the barracks when 'I put my hand into my hip pocket where I was carrying a loaded revolver with the point upwards. The revolver went off wounding my hand, and I do not remember anything after that.'[146] The incident drew the attention of the *Evening Herald*, which reported that the five men had been drinking between 6.30 p.m. and 12.15 a.m. in two public houses, and the shooting had occurred on their return to barracks:

> According to Private Quinn who was walking in front a shot rang out when they were within fifty yards of the barrack gate and on looking round he saw the deceased falling and Private McKenna about three yards away with a revolver held in both hands … The Orderly Officer on being questioned stated that McKenna did not appear to be drunk on admittance after the event but was highly excited and did not quite know what he was doing or saying.[147]

On learning of Leddy's death, Staines wrote to Duggan and identified the indiscipline of the mutineers as being responsible for the tragedy: 'This tragic occurrence is a striking illustration of the state of indiscipline which exists in the Guard since the members, encouraged by those who might have known better, went into open revolt and repudiated all authority.'[148]

RE-OPENING NEGOTIATIONS

Two days after the accidental shooting of Leddy, the Provisional Government and recruits made significant advances in the quest for a resolution to the mutiny. On 24 June President Griffith and Minister Duggan arrived at the depot and sought to negotiate a settlement with the protest committee.[149] Following discussions, the committee issued a statement on behalf of the dissident recruits in Kildare and Newbridge explaining their current defiant stance and at the same time distancing themselves from the anti-Treaty faction that had raided the armoury. In the opening lines, it was asserted:

> A very undesirable state of affairs has existed here for the past seven weeks. The majority of the men, actuated by patriotic motives, and keenly interested in sending the Garda Síochána to the country free from the stigma of having been more or less established, governed and trained in its infancy by resigned and disbanded members of the detested body which had policed the country for ENGLAND, took steps to have the governing departments of the Guard cleared of all <u>STRONG R.I.C.</u> influences.[150]

The statement also criticised the government for promoting an RIC ethos in the new force and claimed that there were sufficient personnel within the country to establish the Civic

Guard without such a heavy reliance on the RIC, which was described as:

> the weapon invented by the English ... to hold our country in mental and physical subjection ... Those commissioned ex RIC could not help modelling the Civic Guard on their own organisation. Their governing positions in the Civic Guard made it inevitable that their spirit would become impressed on the newly born and growing Police Force of Ireland.[151]

Thereafter, the tone of the statement became more conciliatory as, in retrospect, the men appreciated that their efforts to address their grievances could be construed essentially as acts of 'indiscipline'. The men repudiated unambiguously 'the action of the five members of the committee ... and that of their comrades, who have gone over to the Executive Forces, treacherously taking our arms with them'. Furthermore, the men claimed that the anti-Treaty faction within the camp 'took advantage of the extraordinary conditions prevailing here for the past seven weeks', and that the protracted handling of events had presented the faction with the opportunity to raid the armoury. The statement concluded with a declaration of loyalty to the people and to the democratically elected government of Ireland:

> We are, as heretofore, the loyal servants of whatever government may be legitimately elected by the majority of the people. We do not recognise any party, creed or class as being greater than the

whole people. Our loyalty is to Ireland, and we shall serve her through whatever Government she may lawfully elect.[152]

On the same day, Duggan wrote to Patrick Brennan and proposed a three-point plan to expedite the resolution of the mutiny.[153] The proposal included the payment and suspension of all the recruits in Kildare Barracks pending an enquiry, and the immediate establishment of the enquiry already promised by Collins.

On 27 June 1922, Staines was finally permitted to re-enter Kildare Barracks, and he stayed briefly to arrange the necessary pay sheets for the men. The visit provided the commissioner with an opportunity to assess the mood of the recruits in the camp, and the following day he wrote to Duggan to inform him of his visit, which had taken place in the company of Barrack Master McCarthy, Chief Superintendent McCormack, Superintendents Harte, Keane and Neary, Inspectors Meehan, Casey and Duffy, and Sergeant Muldoon:

> I saw, and was speaking to the Acting Assistant Commissioner and other officers, and am glad to say that the general impression conveyed to me was much more favourable than on my previous visits … Supt Liddy TD with two subordinates – Seán Scanlan and P. Kierse, were absent in Clare in connection with the Co. Council Elections.[154]

Staines informed the minister that the required verification of the pay sheets for the men would have to be postponed as three of the finance assistants lodging in the city centre were unable to travel to their place of work because of the bombardment of the Four Courts. This bombardment of the anti-Treaty position by the National Army had started early on the morning of 28 June and it signalled the start of a civil war that would throw the country into a state of turmoil for almost a year, until it finally finished in May 1923.

A stalemate existed within the camp for two weeks as Staines and the recruits awaited the start of the promised commission of enquiry. By early July the headquarters staff had begun gradually to return to their offices and await further instructions. However, on entering their quarters, a number of officers, including Superintendent Prendiville, complained that almost all their personal belongings had been stolen in their absence: 'I found the door jamb had been broken and the lock apparently forced in. I had a good deal of valuable articles there, including underclothing. I had a quite new overcoat I got made in Ballsbridge, a suit of clothes, socks, a binocular glass, tiepins, and many other articles I cannot think of at all. They were all taken.'[155] Having inspected their quarters on the evening of 6 July, Chief Superintendent McCormack, Sergeant McAvinia and Prendiville returned to Dublin by car. Only minutes after their departure from the barracks, Prendiville recalled that they came under fire from Civic Guards:

I regret to say as we were passing down not far from the Depot here going down the hollow into the Curragh some shots were fired – apparently revolver shots – on our right as we were passing down. The poor driver became very excited and put up his hands … They didn't hit the car, but it showed at least a very bad spirit, that is, a bad spirit of discipline.[156]

While the officers appeared intermittently at the depot, recruits became increasingly anxious on hearing the rumour 'that the whole Force would be demobilised'.[157] As the men in Kildare and Newbridge awaited their fate, Brennan took the opportunity on 7 July to write a letter to Collins, in which he put the services of the recruits at the chairman's disposal: 'It is my duty to convey to you the assurance that the officers and men of the Garda Síochána, in Kildare and Newbridge, are holding themselves in readiness for any call (regardless of its nature).'[158] Brennan was eager to demonstrate the loyalty of the men and dispatched a second letter the same day informing Collins that a number of the men would be grateful for the opportunity to transfer temporarily to the ranks of the National Army and assist the Provisional Government in its efforts to defeat the 'Irregulars'.[159]

The secretary of the Department of Finance responded to Brennan's first letter by cordially conveying Collins' gratitude for the gesture and that the government 'fully appreciate the spirit in which the offer is made, and if occasion for a special call on the services of the Garda Síothchána arises the Government will take advantage of the offer made'.[160] While Brennan testified that he never received a response to his second letter regarding the request to transfer men to the

National Army, Staines later claimed that he was personally aware that a letter had been sent to Brennan informing him 'that the best services the men of the Guard could render to the Government at the present moment was to become efficient policemen'.[161]

HOTEL BREAK-IN

On the morning of 8 July, the issue of indiscipline among the recruits resurfaced as Superintendent Daniel Hallinan, a former Cork IRA volunteer, was instructed to investigate the alleged involvement of Civic Guards in a break-in at the Railway Hotel in Kildare town on the night of 7 July. Hallinan was furnished with a bill-head found on the floor of the hotel with the name 'Mr Ring, No. 1'. Immediately, Hallinan went to Barracks No. 1 and met Guard Ring in the hallway, dressed in an overcoat and cap, preparing to leave the depot. Ring told Hallinan that he was in a hurry as he was on his way to meet his sister, who he claimed had recently sent him a telegram to say that she would be at Kildare Railway Station on the 9.30 a.m. train from Dublin. On refusing the guard permission to leave, Ring told his superior officer that 'he was going anyway'. Hallinan immediately placed Ring under arrest.[162] Thereafter, the men of Barracks No. 1 and No. 2 were paraded in front of Mr Connolly, the hotel proprietor, as he had earlier claimed 'that he could identify the men who raided his premises'.[163] Though Connolly failed to identify any suspects, Hallinan continued with his investigation by searching Barracks No. 1, where he found a substantial quantity of cigarettes and bottles of stout, whiskey and ginger wine emblazoned with Railway Hotel labels and hidden in different parts of the building. Hallinan also discovered a large Webley revolver 'loaded in six chambers, apparently left there only a few minutes previous as it was clean and bright'.[164]

On visiting the Railway Hotel, Hallinan recorded a list of damage to the property, including a broken stained-glass window, a broken glass-panelled door and seven other broken panes of glass in other parts of the premises. On examining the lock of the door at the main entrance, Hallinan reported that it 'was fired into at close range, as around the keyhole showed signs of smoke ... and two empty cartridge cases were found outside the door'.[165] During his investigations, Sergeant Doyle told Hallinan that he was on special duty in Kildare town at 1 a.m. on the morning of 8 July and would be able to identify a number of men who had been in the vicinity of the hotel. Hallinan reported the latest development to Assistant Commissioner Brennan and was instructed to place the suspects under 'close arrest', which involved driving around Kildare town and arresting Guard Pender outside a public house. He was also obliged to follow Guard Strickland, the former secretary of the protest committee, into a barber's shop and place him under arrest. When asked if he was armed, Strickland, a former RIC and IRA man, admitted that he was carrying a revolver but refused to hand it over to Hallinan.[166] On returning to the barracks, Hallinan secured the revolver and noticed that 'it had recently discharged bullets'.[167]

At 3 p.m. Hallinan recorded that ten men were under

arrest in the guardroom. Following further investigations, he searched the back of Cunningham's public house where he found two suitcases, one of which bore the label of Guard Pender. On opening the suitcase, Hallinan found a loaded Long Webley gun and ammunition. The other suitcase contained ammunition. When the matter was reported to Brennan at 6.30 p.m., the assistant commissioner displayed remarkable leniency towards the suspects. Hallinan was ordered 'to allow the prisoners out under open arrest and report every two hours at the guardroom'. At 4 p.m. on Sunday 9 July, Hallinan was informed that four of the men had failed to report at the specified hour. He noted that 'their names are Guards Strickland, Pender, Ring and Lynch. They are still missing.'[168]

4

The Commission of Enquiry

On 11 July, Minister Duggan briefed the government cabinet that the commission of enquiry would sit on 12 July at Kildare Barracks. Duggan informed his colleagues that Diarmuid O'Hegarty, secretary to the Provisional Government, and Kevin O'Shiel,[1] legal secretary, were to have been the two commissioners heading the enquiry, but following the recent appointment of O'Hegarty to the position of military governor of Mountjoy Prison, Michael McAuliffe of the Labour Department was appointed as his replacement.[2]

Under the terms of a warrant signed by Collins on 12 July, O'Shiel and McAuliffe were 'to constitute a commission to investigate and report to the Provisional Government as to the breaches of discipline and acts of insubordination alleged to have been committed recently by, and the complaints made on the part of, members of the Civic Guard'.[3] The commissioners were further requested to furnish any recommendations they wished to contribute in relation to the future structure of the Civic Guard. The decision to place the destiny of the Civic Guard in the hands of two senior civil servants was to be one of Collins' last in his capacity as chairman of the Provisional Government. Thereafter, he assumed the position of commander-in-chief of the National Army in response to the escalation of hostilities during the Civil War. W. T. Cosgrave assumed the position of acting chairman of the Provisional Government, updating Collins regularly on important government developments.

THE COMMISSION OPENS

On Thursday 13 July, O'Shiel and McAuliffe opened the commission in Kildare Barracks at 5 p.m. and O'Shiel read aloud the Warrant of Appointment which authorised the establishment of the enquiry. At the opening of the enquiry, Commissioner Staines approached O'Shiel and McAuliffe to inform them that only witnesses for his side were present in the hall. O'Shiel was annoyed that no representation for the 'Men' was available and that Assistant Commissioner Patrick Brennan, 'who had been present in the room a few minutes previously had now left and had to be sent for to his own quarters'.[4] On his return, the elusive Brennan complained that 'the men had no notice of the commission's intention to sit on that day'.[5]

O'Shiel was eager to begin proceedings and asked Brennan to submit a list of witnesses on behalf of the 'Men'. However, Brennan replied, 'I have no list because I take no side. The men have no list because they are not aware of the things into which the commission will inquire.'[6] Brennan also strongly voiced his wish that the 'Men' should have legal representation. O'Shiel reluctantly admitted to Brennan that the requested legal representation would not be available to the 'Men' as 'it would be much better ... to keep outsiders away from it, and to confine it merely to the people themselves ... I understand it is the desire of the Government that the matter should be kept as private as possible. They are not anxious to have outsiders coming in.'[7]

While Brennan reiterated his wish not to be associated in any way with the representation of the 'Men', he persisted with asking O'Shiel and McAuliffe about procedures that would be followed during the course of the enquiry: 'I am trying to get an idea of how this thing is to be conducted. The men are absolutely in the dark as to what sort of an Enquiry it will be. I am not acting for them here. I have not been deputed to act for them.'[8] Brennan persevered with questioning O'Shiel and McAuliffe, and informed them that the 'Men' might be unavailable to stand before the enquiry as they had recently been reduced to the status of unpaid civilians. Finally, an exasperated Staines interjected and took exception to Brennan's insinuation that the 'Men' could be elsewhere during the course of the enquiry: 'Listen Paddy, they were suspended on your recommendation, and they are being paid. There is no use in making a point like that.'[9] Brennan agreed to inform the 'Men' that they would need to submit a list of witnesses and appoint an advocate from among themselves.

O'Shiel decided to adjourn the enquiry until noon the next day and requested that a notice of the sitting times of the commission be placed on noticeboards in Kildare and Newbridge Barracks.

14 JULY

On Friday 14 July, O'Shiel and McAuliffe formally opened the enquiry and were informed that Deputy Commissioner Walsh would represent Staines, while the 'Men' had selected Guard John O'Connell as their representative. A former County Derry solicitor, O'Connell had joined the Irish Volunteers in 1915 and had been active in the IRA during the War of Independence before his recruitment to the Civic Guard. Both men were instructed that they could cross-examine witnesses.

Staines was called as the first witness and began by reading aloud a prepared statement. As commissioner of the Civic Guard, he informed the commission that he was obliged to push 'forward as rapidly as possible' the recruitment and training of Civic Guards to fill the void of the defunct RIC. He claimed that such a task required the appointment of suitable ex-RIC and ex-DMP men to high-ranking positions, as they possessed 'special qualifications for the posts to which they had been appointed' and their 'credentials were satisfactory to the Provisional Government'.[10] Staines explained that the numerous tasks confronting him as commissioner of a new police force had proved 'extremely onerous', and certain officers, such as Assistant Commissioner Patrick Brennan, had failed to support him properly in the execution of his duties. Staines alleged that Brennan's primary duty of recruiting men should have made him aware of unrest among the recruits. Brennan was accused of failing to inform the commissioner in time and Staines claimed that as a consequence he was 'to a great extent ... in ignorance of what was taking place, and which afterwards led to such deplorable results'.[11] Staines claimed that Brennan had effectively and treacherously engaged in a policy of misinformation, and that 'I received the least support from the officer [from] whom I had the right to expect the most – the assistant commissioner – I am at a loss to understand why, but the facts are incontrovertible.'[12]

Staines went on to suggest that Brennan's obstinate demeanour caused a rift between the officers and the men, typified by his refusal to dine in the officers' mess with the families of the president of Dáil Éireann and the minister for home affairs. On providing his own recollection of events surrounding the first day of the mutiny, 15 May, Staines informed O'Shiel and McAuliffe that there had been shouts of 'We'll follow Paddy Brennan' from sections of the dissident recruits as they broke ranks at the parade. He suggested that Brennan was aware that the mutiny had been planned and it was this that had led to his unofficial absence at this time. The commissioner continued his verbal assault on Brennan by suggesting that the assistant commissioner and his fellow County Clare men were guilty of plotting and conspiring against Staines. He submitted a copy of Routine Orders for 17 May, which included the protest committee's appointment of Brennan as commissioner, Haugh as assistant commissioner, Lynch as commandant and Liddy as adjutant: 'The fact that the newly appointed commissioner and the three officers named are from the same County may be merely a coincidence, but it is at least suggestive of much that has happened.'[13]

Staines also drew attention to the fact that even when

Brennan had returned to the depot, he remained with the 'Men' and failed to meet the commissioner at the gates of the barracks to negotiate the entry of his superior officer.[14] Similarly, Staines referred to Brennan's unsanctioned absence on 9 June and informed the commissioners that Brennan had been fully aware that the terms of the agreement reached between Collins and the committee included the return of Staines and his staff on 9 June. He suggested that Brennan's non-attendance implied that he was aware of the committee's intention to refuse the commissioner entry to the depot.

Moreover, during Brennan's absence, Staines claimed, a lack of discipline had festered among the dissident recruits. First, he identified the campaign by Civic Guards to 'injuriously affect' his electoral prospects through the posting of handbills in his constituency on the eve of the general election. Second, he drew attention to the fact that the 'Men' had control of the depot when Rory O'Connor and the Executive Forces entered and raided the armoury. Third, Staines referred to the accidental and tragic shooting of Guard Leddy; and fourth, he drew the commissioners' attention to the recent unlawful entry into the local hotel that was raided by members of the Civic Guard. In his concluding remarks, Staines blamed Brennan and his associates for their alleged part in 'the loosening of the bonds of discipline', which eventually unravelled and led to the disintegration of the force:

I feel that throughout, I have had insufficient support from officers who should have known that the weakening of my authority was the sure prelude to the disappearance of their own, and I think they have behaved most unfairly to the men in not explaining matters to them, and bringing them to a sense of their duty.[15]

In opening his cross-examination of the commissioner, Guard O'Connell questioned Staines about the employment of former District Inspector John A. Kearney at the RDS, and his involvement in the arrest of Sir Roger Casement and the conviction of Austin Stack. Staines sought clarification from the chairman, O'Shiel, as to whether such questions were relevant to the enquiry. The chairman encouraged him to answer, by saying: 'Of course the reasons and the causes for the complaints, and the grievances that exist under the present condition are all within our purview.'[16] Staines said that, to the best of his knowledge, Kearney had nothing to do with the arrest of Casement, and that Kearney was employed by the Provisional Government as an adviser and never as an officer of the Civic Guard. O'Connell then questioned Staines about his involvement in ordering the military to seize the arms and ammunition of the Civic Guard on 16 May. Staines claimed that the officer in charge of the armoured car had been instructed not to take any action until he (Staines) had returned from his meeting with Collins and Duggan.[17]

As the cross-examination continued, O'Connell informed O'Shiel and McAuliffe that the case of the 'Men' would be based on the argument that the appointment of the controversial ex-RIC men 'would give the Civic Guard a complexion similar to that of the old RIC ... The only force that those men had any experience of was the Royal Irish Constabulary, and it was natural, I think, to expect that in the force the same lines would be followed.'[18] Staines questioned the validity of O'Connell's comments by reminding him that Guard Strickland, the former secretary of the committee, and other signatories of the ultimatum on 15 May were themselves former RIC men.[19]

On the conclusion of Staines' evidence, Walsh called on Barrack Master Mathias McCarthy. McCarthy confirmed the amount of arms and ammunition held in the armoury until the outbreak of the mutiny, then described the events surrounding the raid on the armoury by dissident recruits and the confrontation on 16 May between the National Army and members of the Civic Guard. Assistant Barrack Master James Brennan was then called by Walsh to confirm his recollections of the raid on the armoury. He mentioned that he was one of the five men listed by the committee for expulsion from the Civic Guard, and described the rumblings of discontent among the dissident recruits before the outbreak of the mutiny.[20]

In the testimony of the depot commander, Commandant Ring, a detailed narrative was provided of his efforts to persuade the committee to put their grievances in writing in the form of a request. He also outlined his personal struggle to offer sanctuary to a small number of Civic Guards who had been identified by the protest committee as his supporters. He conceded during cross-examination that he had informed Captain Corry at the gates of the depot that the recruits had gone over to the Executive Forces in an effort to compel the military to take action.[21] Thereafter, Superintendent John Byrne and Sergeant Patrick McAvinia recounted the events surrounding their arrival at the depot on the evening of 9 June, and being chased through the streets of Kildare town by Civic Guards and local people until they finally found refuge with a Carmelite priest.

During Superintendent Bernard O'Connor's testimony, McAuliffe eagerly requested that the former RIC man draw on his thirty years of policing by answering a pertinent question. He urged the former district inspector to evaluate the evidence thus far and to consider whether the 'Men' of the Civic Guard could have a future as policemen. O'Connor offered a measured response: 'If the men could see the folly of what has occurred and if certain elements who instigated this were taken out of it I have no doubt that the big majority of the men in this depot who passed through my hands – 1,245 I think – would make good police again if they were properly handled. There is a certain number that may not.'[22]

O'Shiel suddenly interjected and asked O'Connor, 'You think that could be done without resorting to the expedient of disbandment?'

The gravity of the question unsettled O'Connor and he responded, 'It is too serious to ask me to answer that question.'

McAuliffe continued to press O'Connor on whether disbandment or preserving the Civic Guard was the best option in his opinion. O'Connor drew on his own personal experience as a young RIC man and suggested that the dissident recruits of the Civic Guard were naïve in their actions and that they were young enough to learn from their mistakes: 'As far as that point is concerned youth is youth; I may tell you I was recommended for dismissal myself when I had two years service in the RIC and I turned out a good boy afterwards. Youth is youth.'[23]

15 JULY

On the second day of the commission of enquiry, Saturday 15 July, Deputy Commissioner Patrick Walsh presented his evidence before the commissioners. He made particular reference to the fact that he had completed thirty-two years of service in the RIC and emphasised the fact that it was Collins who invited him to assist in the establishment of the force: 'I served in all the provinces, and I had the confidence of the IRA during the fight.'[24]

The cross-examination of Walsh was brief. O'Connell avoided questioning the deputy commissioner about his alleged effort to turn the Civic Guard into a replica of the RIC, or about Walsh's views on ex-RIC men being appointed to high-ranking positions in the Civic Guard. Instead, O'Connell hastily took to the stand himself and presented his own evidence in the form of a prepared statement written by the 'Men'. Though no Civic Guard signed the statement, it was accepted by O'Shiel and McAuliffe as the 'Case for the Men', which sought to explain their actions on 15 May. The structured and chronologically arranged statement included various official documents that had been sent and received by the committee during the dispute. The 'Men' sought to demonstrate their deep sense of nationalist sentiment through an evocative expression of their disdain for the RIC:

> Ever since the Civic Guard was formed a certain amount of discontent has prevailed amongst the recruits. This discontent has increased owing to the number of disbanded and resigned RIC who have been appointed Heads of most of the important departments in the new organisation.
>
> The hatred of the ordinary Irishman for the Organisation known as the Royal Irish Constabulary, is understood by everyone and is condemned by few. That being so, it was only natural that there should be trouble of some kind once it became evident that the Civic Guard had begun to take on a definite RIC complexion. The number of disbanded and resigned RIC who were to be found in high positions gave the Guard an undoubted RIC complexion.
>
> That the trouble eventually developed into insubordination, and might have had tragic consequences, is solely due to the mishandling of a delicate situation by Commissioner Staines, a man whose high and responsible position called for the exercise of great tact and fine judgement on occasions such as the one on the Parade Ground, on 15 May 1922. Mr Staines did not then, as can be proved, deal with the situation in a restrained or tactful manner. Rather, he did, by his method, behaviour and language, rouse to hasty actions the passions of men, many of whom had, during the recent fight with England, faced death and had dealt out death on many a day and many a night.
>
> Commandant Ring (the protégé of Mr Staines) added the divine finishing touch to the handiwork of the commissioner by

endeavouring to incite Dáil Troops to turn a machine-gun on the Camp of the Civic Guard.[25]

In the first part of the statement, it was claimed that the influence of an 'all-powerful' cohort of ex-RIC officers overshadowed the position of Staines and was allowed to fester in the RDS 'despite an occasional small disturbance among the men'. It was argued by the 'Men' that their grievances were ignored at this time and that the ex-RIC officers effectively seized control of the depot and set about moulding the Civic Guard into a force with a heavy 'RIC complexion'.[26] The official appointments of the ex-RIC men to senior positions within the Civic Guard in early May was regarded as the final betrayal of the 'Men', especially the promotion of Walsh to 'almost the highest position in the Civic Guard' on the basis that he was 'a cousin to one of the highest officers in the IRA'.[27] The appointment of former RIC men to the majority of high-ranking positions within the Civic Guard was unacceptable to the 'Men' for two reasons. First, the ex-RIC officers would continue with their policy of transforming the Civic Guard into a replica of the RIC, and such a policy could not operate in a force almost exclusively composed of IRA men. Second, 'these RIC have received a certain training in a machine invented by English and anti-Irish brains for the purpose of holding this country in subjection. The mentality of men who have been pulverised and re-created in that machine is of a particular type and possesses particular attributes.'[28] It was therefore deduced by the 'Men' that the Provisional Government had passively facilitated the promotion of an RIC ethos, and on that basis 'it would have been more honest and less costly on the part of the government to have retained the services of the late disbanded RIC'. The statement questioned the reasons why Collins and his colleagues felt obliged to offer senior positions in the Civic Guard to former RIC men as a reward for patriotic services. The response proffered by the 'Men' was to grant monetary compensation to such men 'if they can put up a good case, for any loss they may have sustained from the date of their dismissals or resignations to the date on which they joined the guard'.[29]

In a section entitled 'Experts in Police Organisation', the 'Men' denied that the government was reliant on the expertise of former RIC men to establish a new police force. The dissident recruits considered themselves to be a microcosm of Irish society, which reflected an 'outlook on things in general of the whole people of Ireland'. The 'Men' claimed to be suitably qualified to assist in deciding the appropriate model for policing the Irish people:

> We have ideas of our own, and we wish to develop and apply them, within reason, unfettered by RIC Rules and Codes and Regulations. To keep the peace, and to enforce law and order in this Nation, it will be obligatory on us to be bone of the bone of the people and flesh of their flesh, and mind of their mind. Otherwise, we shall be foreign to the people, we shall not be able to touch their hearts; we shall be, from the outset, suspected by them, in time we shall be distrusted, and eventually, we shall be ostracised and hated.[30]

It was also argued that, if the government insisted on not drawing on the IRA members of the Civic Guard for positions as senior training instructors, it 'should have, very easily, procured the services of retired Officers of the American, French or German Police Forces, in fact of any Police Force in the world except the RIC'.[31] They maintained it was necessary for the committee to demand the expulsion of the five senior officers in their ultimatum as 'their mere presence constituted a menace to good order, discipline, contentment and application to studies in the Training Camp'.[32]

Thereafter, the statement provided an account of the events that occurred on the parade ground on 15 May and the arrival of the military on 16 May. Notwithstanding the lack of payment and rations over the seven-week dispute, the 'Men' sought to assure O'Shiel and McAuliffe of their loyalty to the Provisional Government: 'Mr Duggan and Mr Staines have been guilty of that petty reprisal against the Civic Guards, who are bone of the bone of the people, and of the true people. And, let it be well noted, despite this infamous treatment the Civic Guard is still rock-steady. It is yet loyal to the Government.'[33] They called on the government to rectify the grievances of the 'Men' and allow them to confidently enter Irish society as 'proud servants' of the people and 'not as the idiotic imitators of the Force which formed the infernal machine called the Royal Irish Constabulary, invented by England to keep Ireland in mental and physical slavery'.[34]

At the end of the statement the 'Men' accepted that the manner in which they attempted to remove the former RIC men was 'undisciplined', distanced themselves from the actions of the five members of the committee who assisted the Executive Forces in raiding the Civic Guard's armoury and reaffirmed their loyalty to the government and people of Ireland.[35]

The first witness called by O'Connell was Guard Patrick Sellars, the vice-president of the protest committee, who had been a member of the IRA since 1917. Sellars was given the opportunity to read aloud his own personal statement of the events that unfolded during the course of the dispute. Sellars explained that the original protest committee formed in the RDS was organised by Sergeant John Byrne.[36] However, Byrne later distanced himself from the grievances of the recruits when he was promoted to the rank of superintendent. This shift in loyalty was one of the reasons why Byrne was chased around the streets of Kildare on 9 June by his former comrades. According to Sellars, the 'Men' gave chase to Byrne and McAvinia following the earlier confrontation that day between Staines and the committee at the gates of the depot. Sellars claimed that tensions within the depot had escalated following Staines' arrival at Kildare Barracks with a greater number of officers than had previously been agreed with Collins. Much to the annoyance of O'Shiel, at this point Staines interjected: 'Now I will ask would I send those men back without the commandant of the depot and the paying officer and his staff, considering the men were not paid?'[37]

During his cross-examination of Sellars, Walsh pressed him on a range of issues, including the establishment of a committee without the consent of the government and the issuing of an ultimatum to the commissioner. Sellars said the prevailing circumstances warranted such unsanctioned action. Walsh then questioned Sellars about the committee's expressed grievance that an RIC dimension had allegedly been superimposed on the Civic Guard and asked him to identify the educational and training policies that had been implemented by the committee since the beginning of the dispute. Sellars reluctantly said that the training of the recruits had continued with the assistance of only two instructors. Walsh asked Sellars if he was aware that the two instructors were former RIC men. On conceding he was aware of this, Walsh remarked that 'when you are sick you must go to a doctor, there is no use going to a blacksmith then'.[38]

O'Shiel said that he found it astonishing as an 'outsider' that the committee had demanded the removal of RIC influences yet 'don't you think it extraordinary that you could then turn around and place some of your men under an RIC man, just the thing you objected to'.[39] O'Shiel questioned Sellars specifically about the committee's appointments of Brennan to commissioner, Haugh to assistant commissioner, Lynch to commandant and Liddy to adjutant. According to Sellars, 'none of them refused to take the rank the committee gave … They considered they were acting in the interests of the men.'[40] This assertion by Sellars contradicted Brennan's claim that he remained neutral throughout the dispute and merely sought to facilitate a resolution between both sides.

On taking his seat before the commissioners, Superintendent Seán Liddy was asked by Walsh whether he agreed with the manner in which the ultimatum was issued to Staines. Liddy accepted that 'in so far as it was a demand I agree it was wrong. It was put wrong.'[41] Though he was appointed by the protest committee as the adjutant during the dispute, Liddy claimed that he only acted in that capacity for three or four days and never researched or discussed the records of the five former RIC men listed for expulsion. He asserted that he only accepted the rank of adjutant temporarily during the dispute to 'keep the men together'. However, Walsh enquired whether his acceptance of the position served 'to encourage them in the belief that they had a right to do these things?' Liddy retorted that if the men had not been 'held together some way or another, the men would probably have gone over to the other side [Executive Forces] altogether'.[42] Walsh then asked Liddy, as a superintendent in a police force, whether he would consider it a breach of discipline to order the men to arm themselves and prepare for a confrontation on the arrival of the military. While Liddy accepted it was arguably a breach of discipline, he accused Staines of enforcing 'British government methods, that is, brute force'.[43]

The conclusion of Liddy's cross-examination involved McAuliffe asking him whether Commandant Ring was 'right in standing by the commissioner'; Liddy said it was probably the proper stance to take. McAuliffe then pointed out that, unlike Liddy, Ring had not disobeyed 'the order of the officer directly appointed by the Government' and deduced that Liddy and his other senior colleagues had in effect mutinied against the authority of the Provisional Government.[44]

Guard John O'Meara was called on by O'Connell to present his version of events surrounding the General Parade on 15 May. The former IRA captain was a central character during the seven-week dispute. In his capacity as a protest committee member, he had challenged Ring about his IRA credentials after the men had broken ranks on parade and effectively placed the commandant under siege for the first few days of the mutiny. O'Meara was identified by Byrne and McAvinia as a ringleader of the crowd who chased them around the streets of Kildare. O'Meara was questioned by Walsh about the committee's criteria for differentiating between resigned and disbanded RIC men. O'Meara stated that:

> if they came out at the right time and stood by the men that fought, I would have no objection to them. At least I think there would be a great difference between them and the men who remained on. They had five or six pounds a week for doing Black-and-Tan work. Surely there is a great difference in the sacrifices made. You could not say there was a sacrifice made by the men who stayed inside.[45]

O'Meara argued that the protest committee's primary objection to the presence of disbanded RIC men in the Civic Guard was that 'the country would look on us again as peelers when we go out ... we do not want to be standing with rifles in lorries, we want to be servants of the people'.[46]

17 July

On Monday 17 July, O'Connell called on Sergeant Patrick Doyle to read aloud a prepared statement to clarify the protest committee's stance towards resigned and disbanded RIC men. According to Doyle, the committee divided all former RIC men in the depot into three categories. First, men who resigned from the force on 'patriotic grounds' to actively fight the RIC and British army were regarded as 'IRA men'. Second, men who resigned on 'patriotic grounds' without pension but did not assist the IRA. The committee advised that 'those cases deserve consideration. A board of IRA officers should be set up to deal with those cases' and on condition that the board was satisfied with the nationalist credentials of the relevant former policeman, 'he should be accepted into the Guards with the same rank he held in the RIC'. Third, the committee strongly objected to RIC men who were disbanded or resigned on pension. The committee was adamant that no such men should be appointed to senior positions within the force and stated that 'we want our H.Q. to consist of all IRA officers', regardless of whether the provision of such men would require their transfer from the National Army into the Civic Guard.

The final paragraph of the statement quoted Walsh's cousin, General Eoin O'Duffy, insisting that the National Army should have a 'Republican' outlook and asserted 'we want the Civic Guard to have the same outlook'. The committee requested that O'Shiel and McAuliffe consider whether the appointment of ex-British army men into the National Army would be tolerated by the Irish public:

If G.H.Q. [General Headquarters] of the Regular Army consisted for the most part of ex-British officers who fought under General Macready the people would think of the Regular Army as an army to keep Ireland in subjection to England. The people of Ireland would think similarly of the Civic Guard if their H.Q. was composed as it is at present, for the most part of men who fought under General Tudor.[47]

Walsh asked Doyle whether there was any 'salvation' for any RIC man, such as the deputy commissioner himself, 'who served up to the last'.

'I know myself I could not have a lot of respect for men who served up to the last,' replied Doyle.[48]

O'Shiel asked Doyle if he was aware that one of the five men listed on the ultimatum, Superintendent Maher, had resigned from the RIC and joined the IRA in 1920 as an intelligence officer and was a Sinn Féin County Council member. Doyle admitted that the committee had wrongly regarded Maher as a disbanded RIC man and was unsure whether the information on the five listed men was 'well founded'.[49] This response from Doyle prompted O'Shiel to comment openly that both McAuliffe and himself believed the 'Men' took drastic action on 15 May without communicating their concerns to the government, and that 'they simply took things more or less into their own hands. You will agree it is an obviously unfair thing to accuse men and take a certain line of action against them – men like Superintendent Meagher [sic], who it transpires, has a very good national record.'[50]

Though Doyle conceded that the actions of the recruits could have been construed as rash, he maintained the official stance of the committee – that it was irrelevant whether or not disbanded RIC men had assisted the IRA during the War of Independence, as their presence within the Civic Guard was not conducive to the preservation of discipline in a force composed almost exclusively of IRA men.[51]

O'Connell then called Sergeant Patrick Coy of County Galway. Coy had been associated with the original protest committee in the RDS, and Walsh was eager for him to divulge whether Assistant Commissioner Brennan or the committee had ultimate control over the depot during the dispute, and whether there was a power struggle between Brennan and the committee. Following a long series of questions, Walsh became frustrated with Coy's vague responses, such as, 'It is not for me to answer that.' Finally Walsh said, 'Well, make it a matter personal to yourself, who do you obey?' The abrupt request to Coy raised tensions within the room. Coy replied, 'As an IRA man after giving seven years voluntary service I deny you the right to ask me that question Mr Walsh. You have taken no oath of allegiance to the Civic Guard or to the Government.'[52]

O'Shiel interjected and informed Coy that he considered the question posed by Walsh to be 'fair' and 'straight'. Walsh did not question Coy again, but concluded his cross-examination by informing Coy that 'in any question I ask I am not a bit personal to you Sergeant. Do not think that for a moment.'[53]

On the conclusion of Coy's evidence, O'Shiel and McAuliffe adjourned the session for lunch, and on the resumption of the enquiry O'Connell called Sergeant McNamara. Before his recruitment to the Civic Guard, McNamara had been battalion vice-commandant in the East Limerick Flying Column previous to his appointment as an officer in the Republican Police. He recalled his arrest on active service by 'a mixed patrol of RIC and military. I was badly beaten by the butt-ends of their rifles.'[54] On answering questions posed by O'Shiel and McAuliffe relating to his personal involvement in the pursuit of Superintendent Byrne and Sergeant McAvinia on the streets of Kildare, Walsh interrupted the proceedings with a seemingly innocent question: 'When did you say you had joined the Guards?'

'I refuse to be cross examined by a disbanded D.I.,' McNamara responded.

O'Connell immediately advised McNamara, 'You had better answer.' Unmoved by his advocate's counsel, McNamara informed the commissioners, 'I am not going to answer. When English rule dominated this country I refused to answer a D.I. and I am not going to answer one now.'[55]

O'Shiel said it was an unfortunate attitude to adopt, especially as the procedures were agreed between both sides at the start of the enquiry. McNamara informed O'Shiel that he would gladly continue to answer any questions posed by the commissioners, but that 'I personally refuse to be cross-examined by a disbanded D.I. I do not recognise him as an officer and never did, or never will.'

O'Connell became exasperated with his witness and asked him again to 'answer the questions'. O'Shiel reminded

McNamara that his attitude 'does not help your case'. Defiantly, McNamara replied to O'Shiel, 'I was one of the first men to object to these men in the Civic Guard, though I had nothing to do with the committee or anything.' O'Shiel explained to O'Connell that he would have no option but to conclude the enquiry if McNamara refused to be cross-examined by Walsh, and then addressed McNamara directly about the gravity of the situation: 'I would ask you, Sergeant McNamara, in the interests of this Force, in the interests of the men themselves and everyone concerned to reconsider your attitude.'

'I could not reconsider that. My conscience would not allow me to answer a man of his type.'[56]

The situation deteriorated as O'Connell informed the commissioners that two other witnesses following McNamara expressed their intention to adopt a similar stance towards Walsh. On consulting with McAuliffe, O'Shiel announced that they had come to the decision to end the enquiry, and that 'it rests with us to make a report to the Government as to what shall be done with the Civic Guard. We shall do that in due course. I must now declare the commission finally ended.'

O'Connell was surprised by the sudden termination and requested that O'Shiel and McAuliffe make arrangements to allow the absent Assistant Commissioner Brennan to make his case before the commissioners the following day as he was assisting the National Army in securing railway lines in County Kildare. O'Shiel said that the commission of enquiry was over as it had been defied by O'Connell's own witness, and 'that a report on the future of the Civic Guard would be sent to the Government'.[57] O'Shiel immediately travelled to Dublin and reported to the Provisional Government. At a cabinet meeting held later in the evening, it was reported that O'Shiel had informed the Government that the enquiry had broken down as a result of the attitude of certain witnesses on the side of the 'Men'. According to the minutes of the meeting:

> He reported that there was a state of grave insubordination and lack of discipline among the men, that, as at present, the Civic Guard could not, in his opinion be organised into a competent Police Force. In the circumstances, it was not now possible to utilise the Civic Guard for Police duties in certain areas, as suggested by the commander-in-chief in his letter.[58]

Following the departure of O'Shiel and McAuliffe, Brennan returned to the depot and was informed by Superintendent P. J. Haugh that the enquiry had been concluded unexpectedly. Brennan wrote immediately to Michael Collins to complain that he had been denied an opportunity to challenge the allegations made by Commissioner Staines in his evidence to the enquiry: 'I think it is only mere justice that I should be given an opportunity of filing my statement with the commission, and also supplying them with such evidence as I have at hand to prove that I am not altogether as vile as Commissioner Staines has alleged me to be.'[59] He made a personal appeal to Collins not to force him to remain 'under the foul shadow of these unwarranted charges'. Following representation made by Collins on behalf of Brennan, both O'Shiel and McAuliffe agreed to hold a special commission for the assistant commissioner and his own witnesses on Friday 21 July, at 11.30 a.m. in Government Buildings. Staines and Walsh were notified about the sitting and were informed that the agreed procedures for the original enquiry would also be adhered to at this sitting.

THE SPECIAL COMMISSION

As arrangements were under way to establish the special commission, W. T. Cosgrave, the acting chairman of the Provisional Government, wrote to Collins and informed him that the minister for agriculture, Patrick Hogan, had already prepared a report on resolving the mutiny. Cosgrave complained that Brennan's demand to hold a special sitting had 'to some extent affected' Hogan's proposals. However, Cosgrave recommended that Brennan should be transferred out of the depot as part of the final solution to the mutiny: 'to avoid possible complications Mr P. Brennan might be transferred to other work. Military Governors for Jails will be required, and as well, an officer to meet the wounded at Railway terminals.'[60]

Unaware that his fate had already largely been decided two days before the first sitting of the special commission, Brennan took to the stand for the most significant confrontation of the commission of enquiry. At the start of his evidence, Brennan informed the commissioners that he would make a statement about each individual charge levelled by Staines against him. The commissioner had previously accused Brennan of negating his responsibility to inform him of the dissatisfaction among the 'Men'. Staines claimed that, as Brennan was the officer in charge of recruitment, he should have been aware of any 'intrigues that were going on in the Depot'. Brennan challenged the accusation and contended that his position required him to leave the depot on numerous occasions and, therefore, 'I was actually more out of touch with the depot than Mr Staines himself on account of the particular job which I had, recruiting … Mr Staines was more likely to be in touch with the depot than I was because he had Commandant Ring to advise him.'[61]

Thereafter, Brennan swiftly dealt with the three charges of refusing to dine with non-commissioned officers in the officer's mess, excusing himself from dinner with the Griffiths and the Duggans, and extending his unofficial leave until 16 May. Brennan took particular umbrage at Staines' insinuation of a County Clare conspiracy against the commissioner on the basis that four officers listed by the protest committee on Routine Orders on 17 May were of County Clare extraction. Brennan asserted that they could not help where they were born, and that the three other officers were appointed by Staines before the dispute and 'not by me or anybody else. His suggestion here is that I had something up my sleeve.'[62] Brennan informed the commissioners that, on seeing the Routine Orders, he was annoyed that none of the four officers had been consulted about their names appearing on the document, and that he challenged the protest committee as to 'why the devil they stuck down our names and why did they not give their own names. The reason they gave was you were the senior officers.'[63] In addition, the committee was eager to align itself with Brennan and his fellow officers, as their presence in the depot was construed by the recruits as an act of defiance against Staines and a gesture of support for the actions of the committee.

The assistant commissioner then engaged with one of the most pressing issues confronting O'Shiel and McAuliffe – the allegation that he had stayed in the depot during the seven-week dispute to support the 'Men' and undermine the authority of the commissioner. Brennan defended his decision, giving two reasons. First, he informed the commissioners that he suspected a few members of the protest committee had ulterior motives and felt compelled to monitor their behaviour. Second, after a meeting in Government Buildings he returned to the depot 'at the request of Mr Duggan and Mr Collins', with the intention of getting 'the men back to normal, to get them to withdraw their demand, and to return to [the] status quo'.[64] Brennan denied that he had ever in fact accepted the position of commissioner during the dispute, and stated that the other officers only acted in their new temporary positions for 'a couple of days'.

Furthermore, Brennan agreed with Staines' observation on 9 June that the protest committee was in full control and that the officers were 'mere ciphers'. This accusation by Staines allowed Brennan to distance himself conveniently from the committee: 'That is quite correct as far as anything concerned with this row went. The committee left the officers to carry on the ordinary training in the camp, but anything in the nature of trying to fix up this business was actively interfered with on all occasions. Not all the committee, but certain men of them.'[65] Rather than colluding with the protest committee as alleged by Staines, Brennan sought to convince the enquiry that he was acting as an agent for Collins in trying to resolve the dispute: 'In my effort to try to get things back to order I was willing to proclaim the committee in the camp if necessary, and in an effort to do so I would have risked all, I might have been shot for it, I would have risked it anyhow because I felt it was my duty to the Government, to the country and to the Civic Guard.'[66] Furthermore, Brennan claimed that if he had not been asked to return to the depot, he would gladly have accepted an offer for his services in the First Western Division of the National Army.[67]

On defending his own position, Brennan identified Thomas Daly as the culprit who harnessed the disgruntlement of the 'Men' malevolently to further the cause of the Executive Forces. Brennan offered his own explanation for the serious breaches of discipline that occurred in the depot and accused the authorities of being unwittingly outmanoeuvred by Daly:

What I think is this, the men's objections to the ex-RIC were played upon by people like Daly. There is another thing, too, that is clear and it is that he used the men's objections for his own purposes, namely, to smash the Civic Guard ... he took advantage of the fight that was there to gain his own ends. The fact that the authorities allowed things to drag along helped them because the men in the Depot began to think they were not recognised, that they were not trusted.[68]

On considering the acts of insubordination committed in the depot, Brennan displayed empathy for the 'Men', who were expected to take orders from former RIC men, who, he observed, were 'walking round smoking pipes with their hands in their pockets. That was because they used to see them up on the balcony smoking after dinner.' Brennan also felt partly responsible for the raised tensions in the camp, as he had informed the protest committee that he had received personal assurances that the services of the ex-RIC instructors in the RDS would be dispensed with in a matter of months.[69]

The early exchanges between Brennan and Walsh illustrated a degree of bad feeling between these two high-ranking officers. On concluding his defence against the numerous allegations levelled by Staines, Brennan informed the commission, 'That is about all I can think of.' However, Walsh hinted that there was some embellishment to his evidence and exclaimed, 'You have managed to think of a good deal.' He then reminded Brennan of his lack of police experience despite holding a high senior rank in the Civic Guard. Though Brennan retorted that he had been appointed by the General Headquarters of the IRA to assist in policing particular areas during recent general elections, Walsh dismissed such a task as 'military police work' and told Brennan, 'You do not know anything about law.'[70]

As the verbal exchanges continued, Brennan admitted that he thought the action taken by the 'Men' was unjustifiable. Such an admission allowed Walsh to enquire whether Brennan's decision to remain in the depot gave the 'Men' a certain amount of moral support. Brennan attempted to side-step the question: 'It may have, and if that is the case, Mr Collins and Mr Duggan are the people who are responsible for my remaining on and for my keeping the other officers there.'[71]

Walsh then turned his attention to the large proportion of County Clare men recruited by Brennan in his capacity as officer in charge of recruitment. He informed the enquiry that one-third of the first 910 recruits to the Civic Guard were from County Clare or neighbouring counties. Walsh alleged that Brennan had exploited his position to ensure widespread support for himself by creating what he termed 'Brennan's sphere of influence'.[72] Brennan responded by claiming recruitment happened to be carried out in his native county 'very efficiently', while recruitment in other counties proved more difficult.

As the cross-examination continued, Brennan accused the Provisional Government of preventing a speedy conclusion to the dispute as it failed to open a proper channel of communication between the 'Men' and the authorities. Walsh said that witnesses such as McNamara, whose attitude led to the early conclusion of the commission of enquiry, would have prevented constructive dialogue between both sides. Brennan took exception to Walsh identifying McNamara as an unreasonable man and took the opportunity to provide his own explanation for the incongruous relationship between IRA and RIC men within the Civic Guard:

... no matter how I disapprove of the methods adopted by the men, I feel they have a certain amount of wild justice we will call it ... that particular man who kicked up that row is a column man and was one of the best column men in East-Limerick. He is representative of a type, you are representative of another type, you will not coalesce. If this thing goes on in the Civic Guard, even though it is fixed up, you will have the same bloody row in ten years. There are two types of mind and they can never be reconciled unless one absolutely gives up, and the stronger of the two is bound to win, and the stronger of the two is that vigorous man.[73]

In subsequent exchanges, Walsh raised the issue of the lack of discipline within the depot during the seven-week dispute. He asked Brennan if he was able to furnish the enquiry with written reports on certain events, which included the shooting of Guard Leddy, the pursuit of Byrne and McAvinia, and the shots fired at Prendiville's car as he returned to Dublin from the depot. On receiving the answer that no reports were available, Walsh continued to embarrass Brennan by referring to the recent break-in at the Railway Hotel and the subsequent escape of arrested suspects from within the confines of a police depot.[74] On exposing Brennan's lack of professionalism during the course of the dispute, Walsh urged Brennan to admit that the grievances of the 'Men' were largely based on their unwillingness to accept the appointment of non-IRA personnel to senior ranks. Walsh put it to Brennan that the 'Men' were aggrieved that the senior positions of the force had not been reserved and dispersed among them as reward for their part in the War of Independence.

Brennan was exasperated and asserted that he was well aware of the reasons for the grievances of the 'Men' as he had been 'stuck down in the damp for two months', and that the dispute would have easily been resolved if there had been 'a proper sworn enquiry with legal representation on both sides, then the men would have a very good case'.[75]

Walsh took the opportunity to ask Brennan if he was being 'very severe on Mr O'Connell'?

'I do not mean to cast any aspersion on Mr O'Connell, not that he cares a damn whether I do or not. What I mean is that the men did not go into the evidence as they should have done, and they did not present it as they should have presented it.'[76]

On the conclusion of Walsh's cross-examination of Brennan, O'Shiel asked the assistant commissioner to explain the nature of his objections to former RIC men training the recruits of the Civic Guard. Brennan clarified his stance by stating that he believed it was not 'right to place them on the head quarters of the Civic Guard'. He asserted that his objections were based on the fear that such appointments would endanger not only the lives of the former RIC men but also the members of the force who accompanied him into Irish society: 'Supposing he went down to Clare he would be shot in twenty-four hours and get all of the Civic Guard shot with him.'[77] Though O'Shiel accepted that such a scenario might occur in the prevailing political circumstances, Brennan declared that 'it will be twenty years before the spirit that is around the country has subsided. It will be ten years anyhow.' O'Shiel then asked Brennan to consider whether it would be possible to establish a police force without relying on experienced policemen. Brennan accepted that he was unable to identify where the Civic Guard could source experienced policemen to assist the development of the force. However, he was certain that the RIC never possessed 'ideal police officers at any time; they were not police officers at all and the argument that RIC men, simply because they were RIC men, should come along to train a police force for Ireland is rubbish because they were not a police force in the sense of which any country understands police'.[78]

McAuliffe asked Brennan about an earlier remark he made to Walsh about the contrasting natures of former members of the IRA and RIC in the Civic Guard. Brennan said that, in his view, the training regime in Phoenix Park was based entirely on 'fear', and that the force had always recruited 'quiet country kind of fellows' and trained them to offer blind obedience to the RIC. In contrast, he claimed that the column men of the IRA entered the Civic Guard fresh from fighting the RIC:

> They came in here; they had been subject to discipline but it was voluntary discipline; it certainly was never the result of fear or pain, it was a higher thing altogether; it was the discipline of Volunteers. I cannot explain it any better than that. If they did anything wrong, say this document which they handed to the commissioner, it was in ignorance. I guarantee that the

great majority of the men there were absolutely ignorant of the seriousness of thing they were doing.[79]

Though he admitted that the 'Men' were wrong to take action against the commissioner, Brennan argued that Staines had allowed himself to be surrounded and advised by former RIC officers rather than availing himself of advice from his former IRA comrades.[80]

In his final question to Brennan, O'Shiel asked whether he considered the recruits in Kildare sufficiently 'competent to police the country'.

'I think if handled properly they would be, but I think if they are not handled properly they will not be.'[81]

FINAL SITTING

On Saturday 22 July, during the final special sitting of the commission of enquiry, Adjutant P. J. Haugh was called to give evidence and spoke at length about his capture by Rory O'Connor in the Curragh. During his cross-examination by Walsh, Haugh was asked about his personal view of the primary grievance that prompted the 'Men' to challenge the authority of Staines. Haugh identified 'the inclusion of disbanded men' as the cause of the dispute. Walsh reminded Haugh that he was a member of the organising committee that recommended the recruitment policy of the Civic Guard to the Provisional Government, and read out a paragraph of the policy which confirmed that recruits would be accepted from four classes of applicants: IRA men; personnel of the RIC or

DMP who had resigned on patriotic grounds; civilians; and finally, former disbanded RIC and DMP personnel. In terms of disbanded RIC men, the document added the specific proviso that 'Applications from this class will be verified by IRA Officers. This may be found impracticable in some cases and in those accepted instances reference is to be made to persons whose opinions can be regarded as acceptable to the Authorities.' Accordingly, Walsh challenged Haugh as to whether he was aware that the proviso was inserted by the organising committee 'to provide for the cases of men whose records could not be made publicly known, and whose records were yet known to people whose opinions should carry weight. You follow now?'[82]

While Haugh denied that he had ever seen the document before, he accepted that the Provisional Government must have been satisfied that any demobilised member of the RIC who was appointed to a senior position within the Civic Guard had received a favourable report from a relevant IRA officer. On conclusion of Walsh's cross-examination of Haugh, O'Shiel questioned the adjutant about the importance of discipline within a police force. Despite his involvement in assisting Brennan throughout the dispute, Haugh said that the actions of the 'Men' were 'quite wrong' and admitted that, from a disciplinary point of view, 'I would condemn the men's action.'[83]

As O'Shiel and McAuliffe prepared to conclude the special commission, they requested a copy of the organising committee's report, Routine Orders, returns on recruiting and copies of all educational and training syllabuses. O'Shiel also took the opportunity to thank Walsh and O'Connell for their assistance throughout the enquiry, and declared that 'things went extremely smoothly' apart from one 'regrettable incident' involving Sergeant McNamara.[84]

5

RECOMMENDATIONS OF THE
COMMISSION OF ENQUIRY

In the midst of a civil war, the Provisional Government urgently required a police force to enter Irish society and placed heavy pressure on O'Shiel and McAuliffe to furnish their report on the mutiny as quickly as possible. By 3 August the government was becoming increasingly impatient and sent a letter to O'Shiel requesting the immediate submission of the report for the government's consideration.[1] O'Shiel replied, saying 'the report is now nearing completion but it would be quite out of the question for either Mr McAuliffe or myself to have the matter concluded, typed and distributed amongst the Ministers ... between this and tomorrow's meeting'. O'Shiel informed the cabinet that 'my work on the report has been somewhat broken up of late by other important business. At the present moment I am engaged in an urgent piece of work for the Acting Chairman. However, Mr McAuliffe and myself hope to have the report in its final form for next Monday's meeting of the Government.'[2] On Tuesday 8 August, the minister for local government, Ernest Blythe, presented a summary of the report to the cabinet and informed his fellow ministers that O'Shiel expected to present the full report within a week.[3] Following the sudden death on 12 August of President Arthur Griffith, O'Shiel delayed the submission of the report to the government until 17 August.

On 17 August Staines performed one of his final duties as the first commissioner of the Civic Guard when he entered the Lower Yard of Dublin Castle with a company of Civic Guards to perform the historic and symbolic task of taking over the epicentre of British rule in Ireland. Dressed in new uniforms and under the command of Chief Superintendent Mathias McCarthy, the guards were inspected by Minister Duggan, who two weeks later was replaced as minister for home affairs. *The Irish Times* observed that few members of the public took the opportunity to witness 'the final step' in the transfer of Dublin Castle to the Irish Free State, as around 100 RIC men (the organisation was not fully disbanded until the end of August) marched out of the gates. An hour and a half later, a detachment of Civic Guards entered and took occupancy of the historic building.

Much to the dissatisfaction of the small public gathering, no official ceremony had been organised to recognise the symbolic significance of the event: 'Many of the onlookers regarded the proceedings with a feeling of regret at the passing of what was admittedly the finest police force in the world.'[4] In the editorial section of *The Times*, the evacuation of Dublin Castle by the last remaining RIC was noted with deep regret from its offices in London. Readers were informed that, apart from displaying 'magnificent physique', members of the force had always been brave, disciplined and naturally quick-witted. Though 'recruited from the Irish peasantry', the editor applauded the loyalty of the force in not shirking their employment duties: 'They were the first victims of Sinn Féin's campaign of murder. The old half-tolerance for the police that had existed during the worst disturbances of earlier days vanished before the cruel teaching of the latter-day Republicans.'[5] While it was accepted that the prevailing political circumstances necessitated the disbandment of the 'best police force in the world', the editor regarded the regrettable decision as 'Ireland's loss'.

FINDINGS OF THE COMMISSION

In the introductory section of the Report of the Civic Guard Mutiny, the commissioners explained that their investigation was 'by no means as exhaustive or complete as we would wish, but, as we have been given to understand that the matter is very urgent, there is no alternative but to present the report in its present form'.[6] The commissioners declared that the protest committee had remained in control of the depot from 16 May 'right down to the 12th July, the day before the commission sat in Kildare'.[7] Summaries of the primary charges made by Commissioner Staines were considered and ruled upon by O'Shiel and McAuliffe:

> That a mutiny of officers and men in the Civic Guard broke out against his Authority in the Kildare and Newbridge Depots. That prior to the outbreak of the mutiny intrigues were going on

in the Kildare Depot of which the officers must have been aware and of which he should have been at once acquainted.

That the Depot was taken over by a 'Committee' of the men who mutinied; and that they deposed the rightful officers and appointed others in their stead.

That all the officers appointed by the 'Committee' accepted these pretended commissions and functioned in the various positions allotted to them by the Committee.

That he received the least support from the officer from whom he was entitled to receive the most, viz., Asst. Commissioner Brennan.

That on the 9th June he was refused admittance into the Camp by the Mutinous 'Committee', although the Assistant Commissioner was actually in the Depot at the time.

That the Assistant Commissioner absented himself occasionally without leave.

That the Assistant Commissioner deliberately absented himself from dinner on the occasion of the [visit of the] President and the Minister of Home Affairs.

That the Assistant Commissioner declined to use the officers' mess on the grounds that the men admitted to the mess had no right [to be] there as they were not commissioned officers.

To each of the nine charges made by Staines, O'Shiel and McAuliffe found in favour of the commissioner. They made special reference to Brennan and other officers who remained with the 'Men' during the mutiny and criticised them for acquiescing to the demands of the protest committee. The acceptance of the committee's legitimacy by Brennan and his fellow officers was considered to be 'about the gravest feature of the whole trouble'.[8] Furthermore, the commissioners found that Brennan was 'at least not as enthusiastic as he might have been in supporting his superior officer'.[9] While they accepted the charge that Staines had been refused entry to the depot on 9 June, they acknowledged that Brennan had instructed the sentries to admit Staines and that the committee had overridden his order. However, on the charge that Brennan refused to dine with the families of the president and the minister of home affairs, the commissioners declared that the assistant commissioner 'displayed whether consciously or not a considerable amount of disrespect' to the Griffiths and Duggans.[10] On the final charge, that Brennan refused to dine with non-commissioned officers in the officers' mess, the commissioners ruled in favour of Staines, but accepted 'that the Asst. Commissioner was within his rights in so acting'.[11] The report did not refer to Brennan's unsanctioned absences from the depot at particularly crucial moments of the mutiny.

In the 'General Findings of the Commission', O'Shiel and McAuliffe identified a range of issues that surfaced during the initial establishment of the force and subsequent seven-week dispute. The section began with holding the organising committee responsible for two grave errors. First, the arming of the force was considered 'responsible for a good deal of deplorable incidents', as arming all members of the Civic Guard created 'a militaristic instead of a peace outlook in the minds of the officers and men' and an affront to the Irish public, who would have expected 'that the day of the militaristic and coercive was at an end in Ireland'.[12] It was also argued by O'Shiel and McAuliffe that the decision to arm the Civic Guard allowed the 'Men' to pursue a settlement of their grievances through 'threats and force of arms, and incidentally played into the hands of the enemies of the Civic Guard'.[13] Second, the commissioners were adamant that 'no elected representatives of the people should have been appointed to any position whatever within the ranks of the Civic Guard'. The commissioners were particularly anxious to prevent personnel with political careers or ambitions entering the national police force, and were eager to prevent any recurrence of the attempted sabotage of Staines' electoral campaign by dissident recruits in Kildare Barracks.

In the second part of the 'General Findings', the commissioners referred to the prevalence of disaffection within the Civic Guard. O'Shiel and McAuliffe noted that discontent was evident in the force from the start of training in March 1922, which was allegedly because of the presence of ex-RIC personnel within the depot who were intent on imposing an RIC ethos on the force. The commissioners empathised with the 'Men' that 'too extensive use made of the RIC at this period taken in conjunction with outside circumstances may have been unwise. Considering that the main body were IRA men, the presence and power of the ex-RIC lent itself to give [*sic*] a certain amount of justice in the view point of the men.'[14] While the commissioners appreciated the claim of the 'Men', they were adamant that 'the *main cause* of disaffection was undoubtedly the propaganda from outside the force, aided to a small extent from within, with the object of smashing the Civic Guard completely or at least rendering it helpless'. They identified a cohort of anti-Treaty men within the Civic Guard who maliciously provoked hostility among the 'Men' towards the ex-RIC members and used their feelings as a 'lever' to generate sufficient antipathy to instigate a mutiny in the depot.[15]

In support of this finding, the commissioners identified particular instances. First, they considered the committee to have been established originally as a 'self-appointed body' on the basis of one issue, the removal of disbanded RIC personnel from the Civic Guard. Second, the committee demanded the expulsion of certain ex-RIC men 'without any regard being paid to their credentials'. Third, five members of the committee, including the chairman, were responsible for the transfer of arms and ammunition to the Executive Forces. The commissioners maintained that the leading members of the committee successfully orchestrated the departure of the headquarters staff by conveying their ultimatum to the commissioner and by subsequently preventing Staines from re-entering the depot until such time that the transfer of arms to the Executive Forces was assured. The commissioners identified the mutiny as the planned result of a strategy devised by the Executive Force: 'We are convinced that the disaffection was caused from the outset by outsiders acting in conjunction with a small body possibly got into the Civic Guard for that purpose, or if not purposely got in, [who] were afterwards brought over by propaganda about the ex-RIC and other matters.'[16] Such an assertion was supported by the fact that the majority of the committee and 'Men' remained loyal to the Provisional Government after the seizure of the arms and ammunition by the Executive Forces. They criticised Staines and Ring for their part in allowing the mutiny to manifest and asked whether the commissioner and the commandant should have asked the 'Men' at the parade to stand with them or the committee. In addition, they disapproved of Staines' decision to vacate the depot and effectively leave Kildare Barracks in the hands of a committee that was allegedly being influenced by the Executive Forces.

The commissioners identified inconsistencies in the committee's ultimatum, which demanded the removal of ex-RIC men because they were demobilised men and had not assisted the IRA during the War of Independence. In contrast to the claims of the committee, the commissioners were fully satisfied that senior IRA officers had requested the listed ex-RIC men to remain in the RIC until the disbandment of the force. The committee issued the ultimatum without verifying the details of the five listed men: the case of Superintendent Maher was highlighted as that of a man wrongly listed on the ultimatum as a demobilised member of the RIC, even though he joined the IRA in 1920: 'The records of the expelled officers and men are undoubtedly satisfactory and a few instances serve to show the misleading propaganda carried on amongst the rank and file.'[17] Furthermore, the commissioners reported that their investigations had led them to the conclusion that 'practically every expelled officer' who vacated the depot with Staines had either resigned from the RIC on patriotic grounds or '[was] ordered to remain in the RIC for special purposes' by prominent IRA officers.[18]

The commissioners were unmoved by the committee's resolve to remove the RIC dimension from the Civic Guard and questioned the relevance of such an allegation, because the committee itself had appointed an ex-RIC man as its secretary and requested former RIC men to assist in the training and education of recruits during the seven-week dispute: 'But we find no evidence of this complexion manifesting itself until after the revolt, and then it showed itself in a most extreme form under the regime of the very parties who allege they were out to prevent it.'[19]

In relation to the officers who remained in the depot with the 'Men', the commissioners reported that their presence offered moral support to the protest committee and their temporary acceptance of higher positions in the depot undermined the authority of Staines and discipline within the Civic Guard. The commissioners also refused to accept Brennan's claim that they remained in the depot at the request of the government to assist in resolving the dispute as 'certain deplorable events had taken place previous to their being requested to return'.[20]

On considering the evidence, O'Shiel and McAuliffe recommended the disbandment of the Civic Guard as 'it is not fit to function as a police force, but is certainly capable of being re-organised and moulded into a good police body if properly handled'.[21] They proposed that each member would be welcome to apply for a position in the new force on satisfying a three-man selection committee composed of an independent government chairman, Commandant Ring and Superintendent Haugh. By agreeing to this, there could be general agreement on both sides that the recruitment of personnel was transparent and balanced.

By mid-July it is estimated that 350 men had departed from the force in the wake of the mutiny, due to their disillusionment with events or in support of the 'Irregulars'.[22]

THE COMMISSIONERS' RECOMMENDATIONS FOR A NEW POLICE FORCE

In addition to the proposed disbandment of the Civic Guard, the commissioners listed eleven specific recommendations to ensure the replacement force would attain the confidence of the Irish public and members of the force.

They accepted the primary grievance of the 'Men' contained in the statement read aloud by O'Connell. Rather than relying on ex-RIC personnel, the government was advised to seek the services of highly experienced officers from America, France or Germany for a three- to five-year period. It was also suggested that Patrick Walsh should be employed in a non-commissioned capacity to assist the foreign instructors in training the force.

The Government was advised to prohibit elected or former elected representatives from serving in any capacity in the new force.

All members of the new force would be appointed on a temporary basis for a minimum period of one year to assess their suitability for a permanent position, and all members of the force would receive a syllabus of examinations to encourage each man to study for the rank 'he considers himself capable of attaining under the examination system'.[23] Through study and examination preparation, it was envisaged that the training process would be expedited, and that the minds of the men would be employed 'in a useful way and take them off other and undesirable things that they appear to have taken to only too readily in the past'.[24]

The government was advised to reserve the most senior positions of the new headquarters staff for ex-IRA men, and that each officer's chief assistant should be an ex-RIC or DMP man with a good national record. Such a recommendation was considered necessary to ensure any propaganda against the new force could have no credence:

> We are most anxious that ex-policemen with good records should be encouraged to come into the new force, but not into positions where they could have a majority voice in directing policy in general. We would strongly favour the presence of at least one ex-policeman in each established station – particularly a resigned or dismissed man who served with the IRA. This man need not necessarily be in charge of the station.[25]

Following a study of comparable police forces in other countries, it was proposed that the new Civic Guard should be divided into three sections. The first section would represent the main body of unarmed policemen and be deployed in stations around the country, as the disarming of the main body of the force would facilitate public acceptance of the new Civic Guard and in the prevailing political turmoil would 'be a safeguard to the officers and men themselves'. The commissioners expected that such a proposition would discourage the Executive Forces from identifying the new unarmed Civic Guard as a legitimate military target.

The second section would be a semi-military detachment of the force, whose members would be trained in the use of arms, but would carry arms only in cases of emergency. It was anticipated that this body of men would be placed under the control of the commissioner and 'be a kind of reserve force at headquarters' that could be 'dispatched to any district in case of actual or anticipated disturbances where the presence of an armed force might be a vital necessity in keeping the peace'.[26]

The third section would consist of a liaison system between local council authorities and the Civic Guard for the deployment of the special armed force on occasions when the peace of a locality was disturbed or threatened.

It was also suggested that a detective force should be established which would come under the joint control of the commissioner for the Civic Guard and the commissioner of the DMP.

The report recommended that a journal should be produced for the membership of the entire force to allow for the publication of useful information relevant to the study of police duties.

A review of the high rates of pay for members of the

Civic Guard was recommended. O'Shiel and McAuliffe suggested that the rates set by the organising committee were commensurate with 'a wealthy country like England'. It was asserted that the RIC members of the organising committee obviously had too much influence in this regard 'at a time when the latter body were practically being bribed with money in order to keep it together'.[27]

In addition to the existing oath of loyalty to be taken by members, it was recommended, after reflection on the seven-week dispute in Kildare Barracks, that the following should be attached: *To obey the orders of all superior officers appointed by the elected Government of the people of Ireland.*

IMPLEMENTATION OF THE RECOMMENDATIONS AND NEW PROBLEMS

On 18 August the Provisional Government held a cabinet meeting to discuss the findings and the ministers agreed to a seven-point plan for the implementation of the report:

That the report should be communicated confidentially to Commissioner Staines.

That Mr Staines should then resign on the ground that he is a public representative and as such should not hold office in the Civic Guard.

That Commandant Seán Ó Muirthile be appointed Commissioner.

That the cases of Temporary Assistant Commissioner Brennan and Superintendent Liddy be then dealt with.

That the Civic Guard be technically disbanded, but not dispersed.

That arrangements be then made for the selective re-enrolment of members of the Civic Guard.

That the Civic Guard be sent out on Police Duty as soon as possible.[28]

On 22 August the acting chairman of the Provisional Government, W. T. Cosgrave, wrote to Collins about the agreed plan for the reorganisation, but the commander-in-chief never received the correspondence as he was shot dead only hours later during an anti-Treaty ambush at Béal na mBláth, County Cork. The death of Collins 'was the great public tragedy – indeed the only *public* tragedy – of the civil war'.[29] At 1.40 a.m. on Thursday 24 August, the remains of Collins arrived by boat at Dublin Port. The animosity that had divided the Civic Guard for the previous four months was set aside as Staines, Brennan, McCarthy and Liddy collectively followed the procession from the port to St Vincent's Hospital on St Stephen's Green.[30]

While the Provisional Government struggled to function in the wake of losing its two most prominent politicians, Griffith and Collins, within ten days of each other, the recruits of the Civic Guard were ordered to vacate Kildare Barracks gradually and transfer to a warehouse at Ship Street in Dublin, close to the new Civic Guard temporary headquarters in Dublin Castle. Within a week, the Irish authorities in Dublin Castle became aware that a copy of a confidential document from Kildare Barracks was circulating among the new arrivals, which threatened to ignite another mutiny. It listed details of the pensions and salaries of disbanded RIC officers in the Civic Guard and was distributed by their former colleagues who had resigned from the RIC on patriotic grounds and so did not qualify for these emoluments.[31] Guard Shaun MacManus, of the accountancy office in Dublin Castle, wrote confidentially to O'Shiel and informed him that there was growing resentment towards disbanded RIC men who were in receipt of both generous pensions and high rates of remuneration in the Civic Guard. In his former capacity as a staff captain in the IRA, MacManus knew O'Shiel during the War of Independence, and told him:

> ... again there are rumblings of revolution over in Ship Street Barracks. There is a general discontentment throughout the force because one can hear whisperings of it daily, and I would not be surprised if the trouble broke at any moment. What it really amounts to is this: the resigned RIC are displeased at the disbanded men having an equal status with them as to promotions – the former have no pensions and that latter have – while the IRA are disgusted that both classes of ex-RIC men are getting all the positions over their shoulders. That is roughly how the matter stands, and I can see trouble if something is not done quickly. If new trouble breaks out here it will undoubtedly embarrass the Government and make for more chaos ... This letter to you is *private* to inform you of conditions here so that you can inform the Government of how matters stand here, and warn them to deal definitely and quickly with the Force.[32]

With the country gripped by civil war and murmurings of

another mutiny looming in the Civic Guard, O'Shiel passed the letter on to the Department of Justice.

The responsibility for rapidly implementing the recommendations of the commission of enquiry had passed to W. T. Cosgrave, following his appointment as chairman of the government on the death of Collins. In the wake of the June general election, the second Provisional Government was finally formed on 30 August. With the Civic Guard already purged of its anti-Treaty members since their departure from the depot with Rory O'Connor on 17 June, the Provisional Government implemented the report's recommendation to disband the force and re-employ the vast majority of the 'Men' under a restructured force.

The appointment of ex-IRA men to senior ranks was intended to placate the grievances of the recruits and to gain the general acceptance of the Irish public. Following the immediate resignation of Staines, the Provisional Government had been considering the appointment of Commandant Seán Ó Muirthile as his replacement. However, Éamonn Duggan had been replaced by Kevin O'Higgins as the minister for home affairs in the new government and he was intent on replacing Staines instead with the chief of staff of the National Army, General Eoin O'Duffy. O'Higgins requested that the minister for defence, General Richard Mulcahy, dissuade Ó Muirthile from accepting the commissionership and advised O'Duffy to vacate the South-Western Command and take charge of the Civic Guard.[33] Ó Muirthile subsequently replaced Emmet Dalton as commander of the National Army in County Cork.

Following O'Duffy's acceptance of the commissionership of the Civic Guard in September, he immediately prioritised both the urgent allocation of guards to the countryside and the implementation of the recommendations forwarded by O'Shiel and McAuliffe. At thirty years of age, O'Duffy had already acquired a reputation as a man of decisive and effective action, whose 'talents were ideally suited to the crisis days of 1922'.[34] Born in County Monaghan, O'Duffy had worked as an engineer, architect and auctioneer. On joining the IRA in 1917, he rose to prominence immediately, and during the War of Independence he was appointed as the IRA's director of organisation and served two terms in prison. While representing his native Monaghan as a Sinn Féin member of Dáil Éireann in 1921 and 1922, he demonstrated his extreme nationalist ideals by advocating the 'use of lead' as a means of coercing unionists into a united Ireland.[35] His appointment proved to be a popular choice among members of the force, as he possessed boundless energy and a deep sense of concern for the welfare of the rank-and-file: 'if anybody could give the Guards zeal and purposefulness, it would be O'Duffy'.[36] Furthermore, his nationalist credentials and successful military exploits ensured that recruits would accept his ideology and his future direction for the new force. Because of the indiscipline of recruits at Kildare and the prevailing political chaos, it was imperative that O'Duffy be a decisive and resolute individual, as he had to impose law and order on a country that had been devoid of a regular police service for the previous three years, and simultaneously earn public support within a country embroiled in a civil war.

The replacement of Staines by O'Duffy, and the departure of Brennan and Walsh from the Civic Guard, brought a sense of conclusion to the mutiny. The Provisional Government overlooked the fact that O'Duffy had been an elected representative and instead decided to emphasise a new beginning for the Civic Guard by appointing Éamonn Coogan as the new assistant commissioner. Coogan, who had previously served as a senior civil servant in the Department of Local Government under W. T. Cosgrave, was quickly appointed to the rank of deputy commissioner on entering the force. Meanwhile, former Deputy Commissioner Walsh was appointed as a civilian adviser in the commissioner's office. O'Duffy immediately took note of what Walsh had earlier described as 'Brennan's sphere of influence' and duly criticised the disproportionate number of recruits arriving at the depot from the counties of Clare, Limerick and Galway, and imposed a temporary recruitment ban on those counties to offset the earlier disparity.[37] In his correspondence with the secretary of the Department of Home Affairs, Henry O'Friel, O'Duffy stated that:

> Owing to the abnormal number of recruits from certain counties, I found it necessary to temporarily suspend recruiting from such counties. For example, in September last, Co. Clare alone provided one-third of the total recruits then in the Depot. Co. Limerick followed a close 2nd on Clare and Co. Galway a close 3rd. This was very undesirable and was, in my opinion, largely responsible for the Kildare Mutiny … It is very desirable that each County in the State should have representation in the Guard.[38]

During late August and early September, the final recruits had been transferred from Kildare Barracks to the warehouse in Ship Street adjoining Dublin Castle.[39] The conditions endured by recruits at Ship Street provoked Barrack Master Superintendent James Brennan to write a letter on 1 September 1922 to O'Duffy. The commissioner was informed that the men were obliged to retire to bed in darkness, and that sanitary arrangements required immediate attention. In addition, 'the food for the men cannot be cooked with the coal. On the 30th Ultimo I took the overseer, Mr Thornton, to see the coal that was supplied – it was slack – but nothing has since been done … Ship St Barracks was in a most awful state when the Civic Guard went into residence.'[40] Rather than establishing a regimented training regime in Ship Street, the crisis of the Civil War necessitated the deployment of recruits at various centres around the city to perform a variety of roles. During his time as a recruit, Patrick Campbell recalls being assigned as an escort to ministers on their way to Dáil Éireann. He was also placed on duty as a security guard at a city centre bank:

> The state of law and order could scarcely be worse with the bank robberies, train robberies, etc. A number of men were armed and two armed guards placed inside all City banks during business hours. Up to this period and until I was sent out the country I must say there was nothing more than haphazard training of any kind.[41]

Similarly, Guard Bill Kelly recalled the disorderly training regime at Ship Street and criticised the government's decision to use raw recruits for duties that many were obviously ill-prepared to execute. Kelly was particularly incensed that the authorities issued arms and ammunition to recruits without adequate instruction: 'When in Ship Street we were sent out daily to the various banks guarding them. Some of the poor devils sent out did not know how to load revolvers. Sending out men untrained in the use of firearms was criminal.'[42] The sentiments expressed by Kelly are understandable, considering the series of tragic incidents that occurred as the force began to appear gradually among the public. In early September, Guard Thomas Bolton shot himself through the heart as he tried to remove his revolver from his vest pocket.[43] On 20 September 1922, Guard Charles Eastwood, nineteen years of age, was accidentally shot by Guard Herde within the confines of the barracks. In his report on the matter to the minister for justice, O'Duffy wrote:

Eastwood was on Guard at No. 6 post – (the entrance from Ship Street to Lower Castle Yard) and Guard Herde went to … see another member of the Guard in this post named Maguire – to inform him that as he (Herde) was going on duty to Killester, he would not be able to be with him later in the evening as had been arranged. Eastwood was on the stairs, and when Herde was coming to see Maguire, the former said 'You're not coming up here Leo' in a joking way, at the same time pointing his revolver at Herde. The latter knowing Eastwood well, and that he was only joking, pulled out his revolver, and pointed it at Eastwood, and forgetful of the fact of its being loaded, pressed the trigger, when a shot discharged, the bullet striking Eastwood in the chest.

He was taken to Mercers Hospital where he was treated, and on the next and succeeding days showed such signs of improvement that his recovery was expected, but I regret to say, he took a turn for the worse and died early this morning ... I went into the matter fully and satisfied myself that the occurrence was purely accidental, and had Herde released from custody. He is most distressed, and on learning of Eastwood's death this evening he collapsed.[44]

Two days later, O'Duffy wrote to the secretary at the Department of Home Affairs and expressed his frustration that two guards had died from gunshot wounds since the start of his tenure. He enclosed a copy of a circular issued to all members of the force demanding that, in future, 'Arms will only be carried by men going on duty, and when necessary, and when not in use, will be kept in a suitable place unloaded ... Should a round be fired accidentally, the man firing it shall be immediately put under arrest pending enquiry.'[45] The commissioner also informed the secretary that 'there will be no further accidents of this nature' as the force was to be unarmed in the near future.[46] A week later, Guard James Green took his own life only days after completing his eight-week training period at Ship Street. The subsequent report stated that Green shot himself with his own revolver at Ship Street. The depot adjutant noticed that Green appeared depressed the night before he shot himself, on learning that he was not to be transferred with his brother during the week to Trim, County Meath.[47]

During the last two weeks of September 1922, the first

batches of Civic Guards were dispatched from Ship Street to County Dublin and ordered to open stations in the villages of Skerries, Dundrum and Lucan. During the initial allocation of recruits to the stations, Minister O'Higgins was concerned about entrusting police authority to young, ill-trained guards, and was particularly anxious about the possibility of inexperienced guards not enforcing the licensing laws rigidly. As a consequence, the Department of Home Affairs reminded the commissioner to impress upon all new Civic Guards the importance of setting 'a good example and that they must, in order to preserve their independence as custodians of the law, refrain from any act which would prejudice them in doing their duty against offending publicans'. The minister was especially concerned that 'young incompletely trained Guards' were vulnerable to compromising their positions of authority in their dealings with publicans by 'drinking while on duty or after hours'.[48] O'Duffy reassured O'Higgins that the matter was receiving his full attention, and that Father Flynn from the Pioneer Abstinence Society would be addressing the recruits on 12 October 1922 and encouraging them to join the society. Furthermore, the minister was informed that members of the force would be allowed to wear the badge of the pioneers on 'their Service Frocks'.[49]

Before their departure to their new posts, as the earliest recruits prepared to take over RIC barracks that had been abandoned during the Civil War, O'Duffy paraded the guards and told them, 'You are going out unarmed into a hostile area. You are the first to be sent out. You may be murdered, your barracks burned, your uniform taken off you, but you must carry on and bring peace to the people.'[50] O'Duffy was mindful of the fact that a bomb had been thrown into Ship Street Barracks on Friday 29 September.[51]

The experiences of the guards in the following months varied according to the attitudes of the local populace. Patrick Campbell was one of six guards who accompanied their sergeant to open a station at Carrigallen, County Leitrim, in late October 1922. He recalled that one night a group of armed men entered the station and lined up the guards with their hands above their heads. During the raid the intruders took personal possessions from the guards, and the raiders, anti-Treaty republicans, warned Campbell and his comrades to vacate the station or face the fatal consequences. On the departure of the raiders, the guards agreed to remain in their positions:

> We stuck it out and a couple of weeks later we were again raided by a couple of armed men. They lined us up as the previous occasion. Some of the gang removed the mattresses from the beds to the street, and sprinkled them with petrol and set them alight. With buckets of water we tried to save them but had to retreat under rifle fire from the raiders. Before leaving the leader of the gunmen warned us that if we didn't clear out immediately we would not be warned again.[52]

During September and October 1922, it is estimated that 1,700 men left the training headquarters and took up duties at various stations around the country.[53] Though the first uniformed Civic Guards entered Dublin Castle with Staines on 17 August, there was no general issue of uniforms until the end of 1922 and many guards of various ranks were obliged to open stations in civilian clothes, their only official clothing being a blue cap.[54] Patrick McInerney remembers completing his training and being one of the first members of the Civic Guard to be kitted out with the new uniform:

After doing the usual slog on the square in Kildare and endless police duty classes and lectures – I don't think that some of us learnt a lot – we were taken to Ship Street Barracks, Dublin … After a few days we were given our first issue of uniform and each was supplied with a light navy blue type trench coat. At this time parties were leaving Ship Street every day for stations in the country.[55]

Recruits were sent to Limerick (50), Ennis (25), Galway (25), Ballinasloe (20), Bruff (20), Monaghan (25), Clones (20), Cavan (25), Kilkenny (25), Roscrea (20), Naas (25), Carlow (25), Wicklow (25), Mullingar (25), Longford (25), Athlone (25), Granard (20), Maryborough (25), Buncrana (25) and Letterkenny (25).

As the parties of guards departed from Ship Street, the minister for defence, Richard Mulcahy, wrote to O'Higgins in September 1922 and informed him that he was ordering the gradual evacuation of government forces from many districts and urgently required the Civic Guard to take up their duties in Limerick, Cork and Waterford as 'there is danger in some places that barracks that we evacuate in this way, will be burned'.[56] This placed O'Duffy under intense pressure to dispatch recently recruited guards who had not completed their training, but he informed the government that between 25 and 29 September 1922 he would begin the allocation of recruits from Ship Street to a selection of districts.[57]

DÁIL DEBATES AND THE MUTINY

On 11 September details of the mutiny in Kildare Barracks were discussed briefly for the first time in public during a debate in Dáil Éireann. President Cosgrave informed the Dáil of the raid on the Civic Guard armoury by Rory O'Connor and his 'Irregular' comrades on 18 June.[58] Deputy Cathal O'Shannon asked Cosgrave to clarify 'whether it is a fact that a special commission was set up to enquire into the affairs of the Civic Guard, and if so, what report has that commission made?' O'Shannon also took issue with the decision to arm the Civic Guard, but accepted that this might have been necessary in the prevailing political circumstances. However, he was particularly critical of the earlier appointment of Staines as the first commissioner of the force: 'It is the first time in my life that I heard of the chief commissioner of a Police Force being a Legislator.'[59]

With no response forthcoming from Cosgrave about the enquiry, the minister for home affairs, Kevin O'Higgins, finally informed the Dáil on 13 September that the allocation of the Civic Guard throughout the country had to be postponed because of internal issues:

The history of that Force, it is right to say, has not been a particularly happy one. There was certain trouble which delayed training, which delayed the time when the men could be sent out through the country. That trouble, I am now well satisfied, is well on the way to being retrieved. Certain resignations were tendered and accepted. A new chief commissioner has been appointed, and I am satisfied that this particular Force will become an efficient and self-respecting Force, and that the members of it will become worthy servants of the people.[60]

Two weeks later, O'Higgins was requested to provide information about the establishment of the court system in the Irish Free State. He told the Dáil that twenty-four district judges had been appointed, but they could not 'be sent out until the Civic Guard are established throughout the country'. O'Higgins took the opportunity to again explain that the recent troubles in Kildare Barracks had delayed the provision of civil administration in the state. However, he applauded the courage of the 'absolutely unarmed' Civic Guards as they attempted to open stations in the midst of civil war, and asked his fellow deputies to appreciate that the decision to disarm the force in the wake of the mutiny was the start of a new beginning for the Civic Guard:

It is an experiment … We have no desire to mould this Force on its predecessor … I prefer to speak of the future of this Force rather than of its past. Its past has not been a particularly happy one, and it is not considered that any great good would come of delving back into the past, drawing up details and enquiring into exactly whose fault it was that so and so happened. An enquiry was held, and certain officers – wherever the fault lay – tendered their resignations, and those resignations were accepted. The Force is starting a new chapter now, under a new headship, and it gives me genuine satisfaction to report to this Dáil that the spirit of the Force is excellent.[61]

O'Higgins assured the Dáil that the primary cause of the mutiny was the successful infiltration of the force by Daly and his comrades, who plotted the destruction of the force by claiming that ex-RIC officers were effectively taking control of the Civic Guard. He also said:

Members [anti-Treaty supporters] were sent into that force to make trouble, to play upon feelings and prejudices of the men, and material was to their hand, and let us say they used that material skilfully and ruthlessly … That particular corner is rounded and that particular chapter is closed. I would like to ask that in this discussion deputies should not attempt to reopen it.[62]

The following day, *The Irish Times* published details of O'Higgins' speech and stated: 'He [O'Higgins] was satisfied that that particular trouble was over, and well over: and, on the whole, what had happened had been a salutary lesson for the men themselves.'[63]

'Fresh Recruits'

During October and November 1922, the remaining recruits at Ship Street vacated the premises and joined fresh batches of recruits at the latest headquarters of the Civic Guard, Collinstown British Military Barracks and Aerodrome, which later became the site for Dublin Airport. The new recruits arrived in response to advertisements placed in the national newspapers on 2 October 1922:

> Recruiting for the CIVIC GUARD being now resumed, applications from Candidates will be received. Attention is drawn to the following conditions:- Candidates are to be unmarried and between 19 and 27 years of age. Minimum height 5 feet 9 inches. Minimum chest measurement 36 inches. Candidates will be examined in Reading, Writing from Dictation and Arithmetic – first four rules simple and compound. They will also be required to write a short composition or letter on a simple subject.[64]

With only huts to accommodate and train the recruits, the barracks at Collinstown remained the temporary training centre of the Civic Guard for the next three months before the use of the former RIC training depot at Phoenix Park was secured in December. A recruit at Collinstown, Donal Colhoun, later recalled the allocation of between fifty and sixty men to each of the bare, cement-floored huts. He also described the inadequate facilities for training at Collinstown, which were often hampered by wintry conditions:

There was no proper place for drill purposes so that squad drill was carried out in the green fields. These were so wet and slippery in the winter months that it was impossible to drill properly or even keep in step. There were two large sheds called 'hangars' which had been used by the British as shelters for aircraft. These were used on wet days for drill purposes and Irish classes were also held in them. Police duty classes were held daily in the huts.[65]

As the Provisional Government struggled to maintain its authority during the Civil War, training and educational standards continued to be compromised by political uncertainty. Consequently, ill-prepared and unarmed guards were hastily dispatched to take over vacant RIC stations throughout the country. John Shaw recalled his experience as a new guard in Waterford city:

I was one of the first party to be sent to Waterford, and I never attended a Police Duty Class as there was none during that time. There was one lecture delivered by a Mr Maguire. As can be expected most of us, if not all, were not aware of what he was talking about and nobody had note books therefore notes were not recorded.[66]

Shaw also recalled the lack of regulations governing the new force on their arrival at an old RIC barracks in Waterford. The only evident attempt to impose some kind of a code of practice within the station was the placement of a notice in the day room, which replaced the title of 'RIC Barrack Regulations' with the superimposed title of 'Civic Guard Barrack Regulations'. Having served in Waterford for a few months, Shaw recollected how he and his comrades were unsure of police procedure and were heavily reliant on an ex-RIC member in the station. On one of his first patrols he apprehended a suspected thief, following a report from a local shop about stolen sweets. A farcical situation developed at the station as Shaw and his fellow guards engaged in a lengthy debate as to how to proceed with the charge.[67]

The inability of the new guards to comprehend police procedure had been considered by Staines only weeks before he stood down as commissioner, and he warned O'Higgins to ensure that an adequate number of ex-RIC men were recruited among the ranks of the Civic Guard. Staines correctly anticipated that, in the aftermath of the Kildare Mutiny, the Provisional Government intended to dispatch raw Civic Guards to police stations without the inclusion of a sufficient number of experienced policemen: 'I could not regard with any feeling other than dismay, the idea of sending units of the Civic Guard to police country districts in their present state, and without presence in each party of at least some member or members of the class of men on whose behalf this application is made.'[68] However, the government decided to rely almost exclusively on ill-trained, pro-Treaty IRA recruits rather than to provoke tensions again through the appointment of ex-RIC men who could accompany and guide the new policemen in the discharge of their duties.

At the conclusion of the Civil War in April 1923, O'Duffy sought to address the issue of ill-trained recruits being dispatched to open stations throughout the country and introduced 'Efficiency Examinations', which each member of the force had to pass before they could apply for a permanent position.

O'Higgins implemented O'Shiel and McAuliffe's recommendation that a magazine should be printed for members of the new Civic Guard and in the first issue of *Iris an Gharda*, 26 February 1923, he included his own personal message to the 'Men', which showed that the memory of the Civic Guard Mutiny remained very fresh in his mind. He informed the guards that it was their responsibility to prevent anarchy from ever threatening democratic government:

> The internal politics and political controversies of the country are not your concern. You will serve, with the same imperturbable discipline and with increasing efficiency, any Executive which has the support of the majority of the people's elected representatives. Party will, no doubt, succeed party in the ebb and flow of the political tide. New issues will arise to convulse the Nation. The landmarks of today will disappear. You will remain steadfast and devoted in the service of the people and of any Executive which it may please the people to return to power. That is the real meaning of Democracy – Government of the people by the people through their elected representatives. It is the only barrier between mankind and anarchy.[69]

6

THE AFTERMATH
OF THE MUTINY

As recommended by O'Shiel and McAuliffe, Commissioner Michael Staines resigned from the Civic Guard in late August 1922, on the grounds that he was an elected representative in Dáil Éireann. In August of the following year, Staines lost his seat in Dáil Éireann in the general election. Between 1928 and 1936, he served as a member of Seanad Éireann on three successive occasions, and was later appointed as a member of the Grangegorman Mental Hospital Board. He died in October 1955.

In his capacity as an adviser to the new commissioner, Patrick Walsh set about assisting O'Duffy and Coogan in the establishment of the new Civic Guard. He was allocated the responsibility of providing the Guard with a strict disciplinary code, which 'emerged virtually as a transcript of the RIC code'.[1] Together, the three men 'steered the unarmed force through the crisis of the Civil War'.[2] On 24 August 1923, O'Duffy made representation to O'Higgins to reinstate Walsh as a commissioned officer in the force, and urged the minister to appoint Walsh as the assistant commissioner on the basis of his contribution to the re-establishment of the force, which had been renamed the Garda Síochána two weeks earlier:[3] 'It is the pity of the world he ever resigned the position of deputy commissioner ... Since I became commissioner, he was indispensable to me. His sound judgement and hard common-sense stood the test every time. The Garda Síochána has turned the corner, and no small share of the credit goes to Mr Walsh.'[4] A month later, Walsh was appointed assistant commissioner and completed forty-six years of continuous service with the RIC and Garda Síochána.

The transfer of Assistant Commissioner Patrick Brennan out of the Civic Guard had already been decided between Collins and Cosgrave before the establishment of the commission of enquiry. On resigning his position, Brennan was provided with alternative employment as an 'officer in charge of communications' in Dáil Éireann.[5] However, he decided to join his brothers Michael and Austin in the National Army during the Civil War and held the position of officer in charge of First Western Command. Before his departure from the Kildare Barracks on 10 September, the recruits presented Brennan with a Wolseley motor car as a token of gratitude for his support during the mutiny.[6] He resigned as a TD on 11 December 1922.

Commandant M. J. Ring resigned and was appointed to the rank of brigadier-general in the National Army. Following the capture of the County Mayo town of Ballina by the Executive Forces in September 1922, Ring and his men were sent to assist the local pro-Treaty forces. However, on making their way past the village of Bonniconlon, Ring was fatally shot in an ambush which had been set up by the anti-Treatyites.

Superintendents Martin Lynch and Seán Liddy remained in the Civic Guard after the mutiny and subsequently both were promoted to the rank of chief superintendent. Following the recommendation proffered by the commission of enquiry that no elected representative should be a member of the force, Liddy had to resign as a TD in December 1922. In his capacity as a district officer, Liddy was involved in the opening of new garda stations, and on his retirement he founded and became the first president of the Garda Pensioners Association, renamed in 2002 as the Garda Síochána Retired Members Association (GSRMA). He died following a road traffic accident four years after his retirement. In his memory, the GSRMA present the Liddy Medal to men and women who have served in the Garda Síochána, but are obliged to retire from the force as a result of an injury sustained in the line of duty.

Other notable members of the force who resigned their positions soon after the mutiny included Superintendent P. J. Haugh, Sergeant Patrick Coy and Guard Patrick Sellars, who joined the National Army. It was O'Duffy's explicit intention that 'no member of the Guard was punished or discriminated against for any action he had taken' in the mutiny, so Sergeant Patrick McNamara, who refused to be cross-examined by Deputy Commissioner Walsh and brought the commission of enquiry in Kildare to an abrupt conclusion, was promoted to the rank of inspector in 1929 and in 1940 attained the rank of superintendent.[7]

CONCLUSION

With the acceptance of the Anglo-Irish Treaty by the majority of Dáil Éireann TDs in January 1922, a new Irish Free State was conceived. One of the Provisional Government's first tasks was to bring stability to a country that had just been through three years of guerrilla warfare against a regime determined to retain its grip on the country. An important part of this task would be the creation of a new police force, as the RIC was, by the end of the War of Independence, largely perceived to be an instrument of British oppression.

Despite this perception, many men in the RIC had strong nationalist sympathies and either resigned from the force during the period 1919–21 or remained in their position but passed on information to the IRA. So it probably seemed like a logical choice for Michael Collins to include those men when appointing the organising committee for the new police force, as their experience of policing was unparalleled in the country. However, this decision would almost prove to be the new Civic Guard's undoing.

As the Provisional Government prepared for what seemed like inevitable civil war, it accepted the recommendations of the committee to establish an armed police force largely based on the RIC model and Collins took the opportunity to reward past members of the RIC with senior positions. In doing so, he failed to take into account the feelings of resentment these appointments would arouse among a body of men drawn almost exclusively from the IRA. He also failed to anticipate how this action could be manipulated by the anti-Treatyites who had joined the new force.

The selection of Michael Staines, TD, as the first commissioner of the Civic Guard was another mistake. While his nationalist credentials as a 1916 veteran and Sinn Féin TD initially satisfied the recruits, he was not keen to take on the role and proved to be a weak leader. His lack of leadership skills quickly became evident and when threatened with a mutiny over the issue of RIC leadership in the new force, he effectively abandoned his position, fled from his base in Kildare Barracks and was consequently unable to regain control of the force. It was left to the Provisional Government to mediate between the dissident recruits, who wished to see the dismissal of all senior officers whom they believed had stayed in the RIC until they were demobilised, and those senior officers who felt they had been targeted unfairly by the mutineers.

While the controversial appointment of former RIC men to senior ranks in the Civic Guard was the obvious cause of the outbreak of mutiny, there was another less obvious reason. Underlying the dispute was a shared sense of entitlement and personal ownership of the force. During the War of Independence, Collins had emerged as the most influential and prominent figure of the hostilities, and he expected his direct involvement in the attainment of the Irish Free State to allow him to determine personally, without question, the composition of the Civic Guard's headquarters staff. However, Collins either underestimated or was indifferent to the degree of annoyance his decision to appoint ex-RIC men was to generate among recruits. Their appointments were regarded as a betrayal of IRA principles and the men were particularly aggrieved by the fact that it was Collins who made this decision, as they had fought for him loyally against the RIC during the War of Independence, as well as supporting his decision to accept the controversial Anglo-Irish Treaty. The recruits were convinced that their contribution as IRA men should have been recognised by allowing them to compete for all the senior positions within the Civic Guard. In their statement to the enquiry on the mutiny, the 'Men' claimed they were a microcosm of Irish society and had earned the right to be consulted about the selection of the headquarters staff. They failed to recognise that such a sentiment was at variance with the democratic right of the Irish people to empower elected representatives of the new state to determine policing arrangements in the Civic Guard.

The outbreak of mutiny was largely attributable to both the failure of the authorities to anticipate the degree of hostility the appointment of ex-RIC men to senior positions would generate among the recruits, and the recruits' willingness to lend support to Thomas Daly and his anti-Treaty faction, in whose interests it was to provoke the revolt. Collins' response to the mutiny served only to prolong and intensify the dispute. He aggravated matters by ordering Staines to continue with the recruitment of another police force in Dublin city, while his reluctance to facilitate an enquiry about the dispute reinforced the notion that he was waging a 'cold war' on the recruits in Kildare Barracks. This allowed the anti-Treaty faction the time it needed to raid the Guard's armoury and defect to the occupied buildings of the Four Courts. The prompt resolution of the mutiny in the aftermath of this raid was probably in large part a result of the embarrassment this action caused the Provisional Government. The promised enquiry finally went ahead and its recommendations were a series of compromises that allowed the new force to distance itself from the legacy of the RIC and eventually become the basis of today's Irish police force.

The last word in this story goes to the first commissioner of the Civic Guards. As Staines prepared to leave his position as commissioner in September 1922, he reflected on the events of the mutiny and issued some cautionary advice to the recruits of the Civic Guard. His prophetic words have since been embraced by the force and are inscribed on a bronze plate at the entrance of the Garda Síochána Museum and Archives: 'The Garda Síochána will succeed not by force of arms, or numbers, but on their moral authority as servants of the people.'[1]

NOTES

Introduction

1   Liddy, Seán, 'Smothered History', *An Síothadóir* (Dublin), August 1962–June 1963.

1: Policing in Ireland before 1922

1   The Civic Guard was officially renamed An Garda Síochána following the enactment on 8 August 1923 of the Garda Síochána (Temporary Provisions) Act, 1923. It is somehow fitting that An Garda Síochána Archives are currently located in the Record Tower, the oldest remaining building of Dublin Castle, which symbolised the epicentre of British rule in Ireland for over 800 years.

2   Berry, Henry (ed.), *Statutes and Ordinances and Acts of the Parliament of Ireland* (Alex Thom & Co., Dublin, 1907), p. 4.

3   Corcoran, Timothy, *Education Systems in Ireland from the Close of the Middle Ages* (University College Dublin, Department of Education, 1928), p. v.

4   Berry, *Statutes and Acts*, p. 254.

5   Maxwell, Constantia, *Irish History from Contemporary Sources* (George Allen & Unwin, London, 1923), p. 9.

6   Connolly, S. J. (ed.), *The Oxford Companion to Irish History* (Oxford University Press, Oxford, 1999), p. 445.

7   Clarke, Aidan, 'The Colonisation of Ulster and the Rebellion of 1641', in T. W. Moody and F. X. Martin (eds), *The Course of Irish History* (Mercier Press, Cork, 1967), p. 190.

8   University of Limerick Law Library, *An Act to Restrain Papists*

from Being High or Petty Constables for the better Regulating the Parish Watches (2 Geo. I c. 10 (1715)). Available at: http://library.law.umn.edu/irishlaw/chron-georges.html#anchor247306.

9   *An Act for the Abrogating the Oath of Supremacy in Ireland and Appointing other Oaths* (3 William and Mary c. 2 (1691)), in Pickering, Danby, *The Statutes at Large from the First Year of K. William and Q. Mary, to the Eighth Year of K. William III*, Vol. IX (Cambridge, 1764), p. 129.

10   Wall, Maureen, 'The Age of Penal Laws', in Moody and Martin (eds), *The Course of Irish History*, p. 220.

11   O'Sullivan, D. J., *The Irish Constabularies 1822–1922* (Brandon, Dingle, 1999), p. 10.

12   As note 8 above.

13   McManus, Antonia, *The Irish Hedge School and Its Books, 1695–1831* (Four Courts Press, Dublin, 2002), p. 9.

14   *A Bill for the further Prevention of Crimes, and for the more speedy Detection and Punishment of Offenders against the Peace, in the Cities of London and Westminster, the Borough of Southwark, and certain Parts adjacent to them*, 23 June 1785. See Palmer, Stanley H., *Police and Protest in England and Ireland, 1780–1850* (Cambridge University Press, Cambridge, 1988), p. 89.

15   Palmer, *Police and Protest in England and Ireland*, p. 91.

16   Osborough, W. N., *The Irish Statutes, 3 Edward II to the Union, A.D. 1310–1800* (Round Hall, Dublin, 1995), p. 614.

17   *An Act for the better Execution of the Law within the City of Dublin*, see F. W. Maitland, *Justice and Peace* (Macmillan, London, 1985), p. 108.

18   See MacDonagh, Oliver, *The Modern Nations in Historical Perspective: Ireland* (Prentice-Hall, Upper Saddle River, NJ, 1969), p. 23.

19   Palmer, *Police and Protest in England and Ireland*, p. 26.

20 *Dublin Evening Post*, 18 and 23 March 1786; see Palmer, *Police and Protest in England and Ireland*, p. 71.

21 Palmer, *Police and Protest in England and Ireland*, p. 71.

22 *Ibid.*, p. 100.

23 Coolahan, John, *Irish Education: Its History and Structure* (Institute of Public Administration, Dublin, 1981), p. 3.

24 Boyle, Kevin, 'Police in Ireland before the Union III', *Irish Jurist*, Vol. XI, 1973, p. 342.

25 Brewer, John D., *The Royal Irish Constabulary: An Oral History* (Institute of Irish Studies, Belfast, 1990), p. 3.

26 O'Sullivan, *The Irish Constabularies*, p. 32.

27 *The Leinster Constabulary Barrack Regulations*; see Palmer, *Police and Protest in England and Ireland*, p. 260.

28 Palmer, *Police and Protest in England and Ireland*, p. 260.

29 *Ibid.*, p. 252.

30 *Ibid.*, p. 332.

31 *Ibid.*, p. 362.

32 O'Sullivan, *The Irish Constabularies*, p. 61.

33 *Constabulary List & Directory* (Dublin: 1844) (Haliday/No. 1899, Royal Irish Academy), p. 148.

34 Coolahan, *Irish Education*, p. 12.

35 *Annual Reports of the Commissioners of National Education for Ireland, 1831–1870.*

36 O'Sullivan, *The Irish Constabularies*, p. 44.

37 Kohl, Johann Georg, *Ireland* (Harper & Brothers, New York, 1844), p. 143.

38 Shaw-Kennedy, James, *Standing Rules and Regulations for the Government and Guidance of the Constabulary Force of Ireland* (Dublin, 1837).

39 O'Sullivan, *The Irish Constabularies*, p. 148.

40 Shaw-Kennedy, *Standing Rules and Regulations*, para. 96.

See also Head, Francis, *A Fortnight in Ireland* (John Murray, London, 1852), p. 53.

41   Blake, H. A., 'The Irish Police', *The Nineteenth Century*, Vol. IX, No. 48, 1881, p. 390.

42   Lowe, W. J. and Malcolm, E. L. 'The Domestication of the RIC 1836–1922', *Irish Economic and Social History*, Vol. XIX, 1992, p. 29.

43   Herlihy, Jim, *The Dublin Metropolitan Police: A Short History and Genealogical Guide, 1836–1925* (Four Courts Press, Dublin, 2001), p. 20.

44   Connolly (ed.), *The Oxford Companion to Irish History*, p. 229.

45   Daly, Mary, *The Famine in Ireland* (Dundalk: Dublin Historical Association, 1986), p. 110.

46   Connolly (ed.), *The Oxford Companion to Irish History*, p. 229.

47   Breathnach, Seamus, *The Irish Police: From Earliest Times to the Present Day* (Anvil Books, Dublin, 1974), p. 48.

48   See Curtis, Robert, *The History of the Royal Irish Constabulary* (McGlashan & Gill, London, 1871), p. 182.

49   See Breathnach, *The Irish Police*, p. 59.

50   Moody, T. W., 'Fenianism, Home Rule and the Land War', in Moody and Martin (eds), *The Course of Irish History*, p. 286.

51   O'Sullivan, *The Irish Constabularies*, p. 158.

52   de Búrca, Marcus, *The GAA: A History* (Gill & Macmillan, Dublin, 1999), p. 53.

53   O'Sullivan, *The Irish Constabularies*, p. 226.

54   *Ibid.*, p. 227.

55   See Herlihy, Jim, *The Royal Irish Constabulary: A Short History and Genealogical Guide* (Four Courts Press, Dublin, 1997), p. 59.

56   *RIC Police Code*, 1909; see Herlihy, *The Royal Irish Constabulary*, p. 80.

57   Herlihy, *The Royal Irish Constabulary*, p. 86.

58   Vernon, R. V., Under Secretary of State, Colonial Office to the Secretary of State, Colonial Office, London, May 11, 1905, *Report on the Training and Organisation of the Royal Irish Constabulary* (NAUK, CO 884/9/3), p. 3.

59   Sparrow, Robert, 'The Training of Colonial Police Officers at the RIC Depot, Phoenix Park, Dublin', *The Royal Irish Constabulary Magazine*, Vol. 1, No. 4, February 1912, p. 115.

60   See Dorothy Macardle, *The Irish Republic* (Irish Press, Dublin, 1951), p. 6.

61   Lee, J. J., *Ireland 1912–1985* (Cambridge University Press, Cambridge, 1990), p. 18.

62   See Robinson, Lennox, *Lady Gregory's Journals* (Putnam, London, 1946), p. 170.

63   Gaughan, J. A. (ed.), *Memoirs of Constable Jeremiah Mee, RIC* (Mercier Press, Cork, 2012), p. 50.

64   Fitzpatrick, David, *Politics and Irish Life, 1913–1921* (Gill & Macmillan, Dublin, 1977), p. 6.

65   Lee, *Ireland 1912–1985*, p. 8.

66   *Ibid.*, p. 38.

67   Elected Irish MPs who recognised the legitimacy of Dáil Éireann referred to themselves as TDs (*Teachta Dála* – members of Dáil Éireann).

68   Lyons, F. S. L., *Ireland Since the Famine* (Fontana, London, 1980), p. 400.

69   Coogan, Tim Pat, *The IRA* (HarperCollins, London, 1995), p. 24.

70   Breen, Dan, *My Fight for Irish Freedom* (Anvil Books, Dublin, 1981), p. 32.

71   Hopkinson, Michael, *The Irish War of Independence* (Gill & Macmillan, Dublin, 2004), p. 201.

72   See Macardle, *The Irish Republic*, p. 289.

73 See Holt, Edgar, *Protest in Arms: The Irish Troubles, 1916–1923* (Putnam, London, 1960), p. 171.

74 *Ibid.*, p. 179.

75 *Ibid.*

76 See Fitzpatrick, *Politics and Irish Life*, p. 10.

77 Shea, Patrick, *Voices and the Sound of Drums: An Irish Autobiography* (Blackstaff Press, Belfast, 1981), p. 22.

78 Brewer, *The Royal Irish Constabulary*, p. 9.

79 Middlemas, Keith (ed.), *Thomas Jones' Whitehall Diary, Ireland 1918–1925*, extracts from, Vol. III (Oxford University Press, London, 1971), p. 17.

80 See Mitchell, Arthur, *Revolutionary Government in Ireland* (Gill & Macmillan, Dublin, 1995), p. 202.

81 See Charles Townshend, *The British Campaign in Ireland, 1919–1921* (Oxford: Clarendon Press, 1975), p. 94.

82 Gaughan (ed.), *The Memoirs of Constable Jeremiah Mee, RIC*, p. 96.

83 *Ibid.*, pp. 140–1.

84 Hopkinson, *The Irish War of Independence*, p. 40.

85 Brady, Conor, *Guardians of the Peace* (2nd edn) (Prendeville Publishing, London, 2000), p. 23.

86 See Jones, *Whitehall Diary*, Vol. III, p. 24.

87 See Brady, *Guardians of the Peace*, p. 26.

2: The Replacement of the RIC

1 See Macardle, *The Irish Republic*, pp. 512–13.

2 Oath of Allegiance, Article 17, as included in the Constitution of the Irish Free State, 1922: 'I … do solemnly swear true faith and allegiance to the Constitution of the Irish Free State as by law established, and that I will be faithful to H.M. King George V, his heirs and successors by law in virtue of the common

citizenship of Ireland with Great Britain and her adherence to and membership of the group of nations forming the British Commonwealth of nations.'

3   In April 1923, the pro-Treaty Sinn Féin section of the party established its own separate political party, Cumann na nGaedheal ('Party of the Irish').

4   Lee, *Ireland 1912–1985*, p. 54.

5   Brady, *Guardians of the Peace*, p. 34.

6   Abbot, Richard, *Police Casualties in Ireland 1919–1922* (Mercier Press, Cork, 2000), pp. 271–8.

7   See Brady, *Guardians of the Peace*, p. 35.

8   Allen, Gregory, *The Garda Síochána: Policing Independent Ireland, 1922–1982* (Gill & Macmillan, Dublin, 1999), p. 14.

9   Michael Collins to Patrick Walsh, 3 February 1922 (Patrick Walsh Papers, Garda Museum and Archives [hereafter GM, Walsh Papers]). See also D. J. O'Sullivan, *District Inspector John A. Kearney* (Trafford Publishing, Bloomington, IN, 2005), p. 93.

10   Evidence of Superintendent Jeremiah Maher [hereafter Evidence of Maher], 15 July 1922, in 'Minutes of Evidence of the Commission of Enquiry into the Civic Guard following the Mutiny of 1922' [hereafter Minutes of Evidence to Mutiny Enquiry] (National Archives of Ireland [hereafter NAI], Department of Justice [hereafter D/J] H235/329).

11   See Allen, *The Garda Síochána*, pp. 15–16.

12   'Report of Police Organisation Committee', 27 February 1922 [hereafter Organising Committee Report] (NAI, Department of the Taoiseach [hereafter D/T] S9049A).

13   'Report on Conditions at Rath Internment Camp', 1921 (NAI, Department of Finance 2/304-6).

14   Brady, *Guardians of the Peace*, p. 37.

15 'Organising Committee Report', 27 February 1922 (NAI, D/T, S9049A).

16 *Ibid.*, p. 7.

17 Brady, *Guardians of the Peace*, p. 38.

18 'Organising Committee Report', 27 February 1922 (NAI, D/T, S9049A), p. 1.

19 *Ibid.*, p. 3.

20 *Ibid.*, p. 7.

21 'Preparations for next week's big show', *The Irish Times*, 9 May 1922, p. 6.

22 Éamonn Coogan, Assistant Commissioner, to Henry O'Friel, Secretary of Department of Home Affairs, 29 May 1922 (NAI, D/J, H99/174).

23 See Allen, *The Garda Síochána*, p. 23.

24 Evidence of Superintendent Bernard O'Connor, 14 July 1922, in Minutes of Evidence to Mutiny Enquiry.

25 'New police force: Training at Ballsbridge', *The Irish Times*, 8 March 1922, p. 6.

26 'The Irish Civic Guard', *The Irish Times*, 10 March 1922, p. 6.

27 McNiffe, Liam, *A History of the Garda Síochána* (Wolfhound, Dublin, 1997), p. 18.

28 Recollections of Patrick Campbell, 1977–8 (Shaw Papers, privately held papers of former Sergeant John Shaw, Portarlington, County Laois).

29 Edward Bohane, Director of RDS, to Minister Éamonn Duggan, 20 February 1922 (NAI, D/J, H99/10).

30 See McNiffe, *A History of the Garda Síochána*, p. 58.

31 Recollections of Campbell, 1977–8 (Shaw Papers).

32 *Ibid.*

33 Evidence of Commissioner Michael Staines, TD [hereafter Evidence of Staines], 14 July 1922, in Minutes of Evidence to

Mutiny Enquiry.

34   *Ibid.*

35   Evidence of Superintendent Seán Liddy, TD [hereafter Evidence of Liddy], 15 July 1922, in Minutes of Evidence to Mutiny Enquiry.

36   Brennan, Michael, *The War in Clare, 1911–1921* (Four Courts Press and Irish Academic Press, Dublin, 1980), p. 13.

37   *Ibid.*, p. 36.

38   Evidence of Assistant Commissioner Patrick Brennan, TD [hereafter Evidence of P. Brennan], 21 July 1922, in Minutes of Evidence to Mutiny Enquiry.

39   Liddy, 'Smothered History', August 1962, p. 30.

40   Evidence of Commandant Michael Ring [hereafter Evidence of Ring], 14 July 1922, in Minutes of Evidence to Mutiny Enquiry.

41   Brigadier General Percy French Crozier [hereafter Crozier] to Minister for Local Government, W. T. Cosgrave, 1 January 1922 (NAI, D/J, H99/2).

42   Henry O'Friel, Secretary of the Department of Home Affairs to Crozier, 7 April 1922 (NAI, D/J, H99/2).

43   Evidence of P. Brennan, 21 July 1922, in Minutes of Evidence to Mutiny Enquiry.

44   Evidence of Staines, 14 July 1922, in Minutes of Evidence to Mutiny Enquiry.

45   Austin Stack, TD, Dáil Éireann Debates, 28 February 1922, Vol. 2, Col. 118; see Office of the Houses of the Oireachtas, available at debates.oireachtas.ie.

46   Liddy, 'Smothered History', August 1962, p. 31.

47   The first Protest Committee comprised fourteen men, according to Evidence of Guard John O'Meara [hereafter Evidence of O'Meara], 15 July 1922, in Minutes of Evidence to Mutiny Enquiry.

48 Evidence of Sergeant Thomas Kilroy [hereafter Evidence of Kilroy], 17 July 1922, in Minutes of Evidence to Mutiny Enquiry.

49 Evidence of O'Meara, 15 July 1922, in Minutes of Evidence to Mutiny Enquiry.

50 Evidence of Sergeant Patrick McNamara [hereafter Evidence of McNamara], 17 July 1922 in Minutes of Evidence to Mutiny Enquiry.

51 Evidence of Sergeant Patrick Coy [hereafter Evidence of Coy], 17 July 1922, in Minutes of Evidence to Mutiny Enquiry.

52 *Ibid.*

53 Evidence of Kilroy, 17 July 1922, in Minutes of Evidence to Mutiny Enquiry.

54 *Ibid.*

55 Evidence of P. Brennan, 21 July 1922, in Minutes of Evidence to Mutiny Enquiry.

56 *Ibid.*

57 *Ibid.*

58 *Ibid.*

59 Evidence of Kilroy, 21 July 1922, in Minutes of Evidence to Mutiny Enquiry.

60 *Ibid.*

61 O'Sullivan, *District Inspector John A. Kearney*, p. 179.

62 'All IRA Men Except 30', *The Irish Times*, 25 March 1922, p. 6.

63 'Defiant IRA: Convention Held', *The Irish Times*, 27 March 1922, p. 5.

64 'Crisis in the IRA: Rival Authorities', *The Irish Times*, 29 March 1922, p. 5.

65 *Ibid.*

66 Evidence of P. Brennan, 21 July 1922, in Minutes of Evidence to Mutiny Enquiry.

67 O'Sullivan, *District Inspector John A. Kearney*, p. 194.

68 Allen, *The Garda Síochána*, p. 30.

69 Evidence of Staines, 14 June 1922, in Minutes of Evidence to Mutiny Enquiry.

70 Padraig Ó Dubhaoinrigh, written attestation to the assistance given to the IRA by John Kearney during the War of Independence, June 1922 (University College Dublin Archives, Desmond Fitzgerald Papers).

71 Lieutenant Colonel Geoffrey Trollope, 'Take It or Leave It', unpublished memoirs, Essex Regiment Museum, Chelmsford, Essex.

72 Evidence of P. Brennan, 21 July 1922, in Minutes of Evidence to Mutiny Enquiry.

73 Liddy, 'Smothered History', August 1962, p. 32.

74 *Ibid.*

75 *Ibid.*, p. 33.

76 'IRA cleavage', *The Irish Times*, 7 April 1922, p. 5.

77 'Shot by armed raiders', *The Irish Times*, 11 April 1922, p. 6.

78 Liddy, 'Smothered History', August 1962, p. 33.

79 'Army and Unity: Four Courts Terms', *The Irish Times*, 22 April 1922, p. 5.

80 'Mr O'Connor talks: The seizure and the situation', *The Irish Times*, 15 April 1922, p. 7.

81 Staines to Duggan, 11 April 1922 (NAI, D/J, H99/10).

82 Bohane to Duggan, 4 April 1922 (NAI, D/J, H99/10).

83 Evidence of Barrack Master Mathias McCarthy [hereafter McCarthy], 14 July 1922, in Minutes of Evidence to Mutiny Enquiry.

84 Recollections of John Moore 1976 (Shaw Papers).

85 Brady, *Guardians of the Peace*, p. 53.

86 Evidence of Mr J. A. O'Connell, 14 July 1922, in Minutes of Evidence to Mutiny Enquiry.

87 'Case for the Men', statement read out by J. A. O'Connell on behalf of the Civic Guards, 14 July 1922, Minutes of Evidence to Mutiny Enquiry.

88 List of appointments to headquarters staff in the Civic Guard, May 1922 (NAI, D/J, H235/329).

89 Evidence of Superintendent James Brennan [hereafter Evidence of J. Brennan], 14 July 1922, in Minutes of Evidence to Mutiny Enquiry.

90 Evidence of Staines, 14 July 1922, in Minutes of Evidence to Mutiny Enquiry, p. 3.

91 Evidence of P. Brennan, 21 July 1922, in Minutes of Evidence to Mutiny Enquiry.

92 *Ibid.*

93 Cross-examination of Brennan by Walsh, 21 July 1922, in Minutes of Evidence to Mutiny Enquiry.

94 Evidence of Staines, 14 July 1922, in Minutes of Evidence to Mutiny Enquiry.

95 Evidence of P. Brennan, 21 July 1922, in Minutes of Evidence to Mutiny Enquiry.

96 *Ibid.*

97 Evidence of Staines, 14 July 1922, in Minutes of Evidence to Mutiny Enquiry.

3: The Outbreak of Mutiny

1 'Case for the Men', statement read by Guard J. A. O'Connell, 15 July 1922, in Minutes of Evidence to Mutiny Enquiry.

2 Evidence of Staines, 14 July 1922, in Minutes of Evidence to Mutiny Enquiry.

3 'Case for the Men', statement read by Guard J. A. O'Connell, 15 July 1922, in Minutes of Evidence to Mutiny Enquiry.

4 Staines to Duggan, 16 May 1922 (GM, Walsh Papers).

5   Allen, *The Garda Síochána*, p. 14.

6   See Introduction to Eoin O'Duffy Papers, Collection List Number 166, National Library of Ireland, November 2010, p. 3.

7   *Ibid.*, p. 2.

8   See Allen, *The Garda Síochána*, p. 240.

9   Evidence of Maher, 15 July 1922, in Minutes of Evidence to Mutiny Enquiry.

10 *Ibid.*

11 Evidence of Superintendent Prendiville [hereafter Evidence of Prendiville], 15 July 1922, in Minutes of Evidence to Mutiny Enquiry.

12 *Ibid.*

13 *Ibid.*

14 Evidence of J. Brennan, 14 July 1922, in Minutes of Evidence to Mutiny Enquiry.

15 Evidence of O'Connor, 14 July 1922, in Minutes of Evidence to Mutiny Enquiry.

16 *Ibid.*

17 Evidence of Staines, 14 July 1922, in Minutes of Evidence to Mutiny Enquiry.

18 *Ibid.*

19 Evidence of Ring, 14 July 1922, in Minutes of Evidence to Mutiny Enquiry.

20 'Case for the Men', statement read out by J. A. O'Connell on behalf of the Civic Guards, 15 July 1922, in Minutes of Evidence to Mutiny Enquiry.

21 Evidence of Liddy, 15 July 1922, in Minutes of Evidence to Mutiny Enquiry.

22 'Case for the Men', statement read out by J. A. O'Connell on behalf of the Civic Guards, 15 July 1922, in Minutes of Evidence to Mutiny Enquiry.

23 Evidence of Liddy, 15 July 1922, in Minutes of Evidence to Mutiny Enquiry.

24 Evidence of Staines, 14 July 1922, in Minutes of Evidence to Mutiny Enquiry.

25 *Ibid.*

26 *Ibid.*

27 Evidence of P. Brennan, 21 July 1922, in Minutes of Evidence to Mutiny Enquiry.

28 *Ibid.*

29 *Ibid.*

30 'Case for the Men', statement read out by J. A. O'Connell on behalf of the Civic Guards, 15 July 1922, in Minutes of Evidence to Mutiny Enquiry.

31 Evidence of Ring, 14 July 1922, in Minutes of Evidence to Mutiny Enquiry.

32 *Ibid.*

33 *Ibid.*

34 *Ibid.*

35 'Case for the Men', statement read out by J. A. O'Connell on behalf of the Civic Guards, 15 July 1922, in Minutes of Evidence to Mutiny Enquiry.

36 Evidence of McCarthy, 14 July 1922, in Minutes of Evidence to Mutiny Enquiry.

37 *Ibid.*

38 Liddy, 'Smothered History', December 1962, p. 29.

39 Evidence of O'Meara, 15 July 1922, in Minutes of Evidence to Mutiny Enquiry.

40 'Case for the Men', statement read out by J. A. O'Connell on behalf of the Civic Guards, 15 July 1922, in Minutes of Evidence to Mutiny Enquiry.

41 Evidence of Ring, 14 July 1922, in Minutes of Evidence to

Mutiny Enquiry.

42 Evidence of Staines, 14 July 1922, in Minutes of Evidence to Mutiny Enquiry.

43 *Ibid.*

44 'Commission of Enquiry, Facts, Charges and Counter-Charges', August 1922 (NAI, D/T, S9048), p. 15.

45 Evidence of Superintendent John Joseph Byrne [hereafter Evidence of Byrne], 14 July 1922, in Minutes of Evidence to Mutiny Enquiry.

46 Staines to Duggan, 16 May 1922 (GM, Walsh Papers).

47 Evidence of Ring, 14 July 1922, in Minutes of Evidence to Mutiny Enquiry.

48 Evidence of Guard Patrick Sellars [Evidence of Sellars], 15 July 1922, in Minutes of Evidence to Mutiny Enquiry.

49 Evidence of Byrne, 14 July 1922, in Minutes of Evidence to Mutiny Enquiry.

50 Evidence of Ring, 14 July 1922, in Minutes of Evidence to Mutiny Enquiry.

51 *Ibid.*

52 *Ibid.*

53 'Case for the Men', statement read out by J. A. O'Connell on behalf of the Civic Guards, 15 July 1922, in Minutes of Evidence to Mutiny Enquiry.

54 Evidence of Liddy, 15 July 1922, in Minutes of Evidence to Mutiny Enquiry.

55 Liddy, 'Smothered History', December 1962, p. 31.

56 Evidence of Liddy, 15 July 1922, in Minutes of Evidence to Mutiny Enquiry.

57 Donohue, James, 'Depot Days at Kildare', *Garda Review* [hereafter Donohue, 'Depot Days at Kildare'], July 1948, p. 617.

58 Evidence of O'Connor, 14 July 1922, in Minutes of Evidence to Mutiny Enquiry.

59 *Ibid.*

60 Evidence of P. Brennan, 21 July 1922, in Minutes of Evidence to Mutiny Enquiry.

61 'Case for the Men', statement read out by J. A. O'Connell on behalf of the Civic Guards, 15 July 1922, in Minutes of Evidence to Mutiny Enquiry.

62 Evidence of Staines, 14 July 1922, in Minutes of Evidence to Mutiny Enquiry.

63 Evidence of P. Brennan, 21 July 1922, in Minutes of Evidence to Mutiny Enquiry.

64 Evidence of Staines, 14 July 1922, in Minutes of Evidence to Mutiny Enquiry.

65 Evidence of P. Brennan, 21 July 1922, in Minutes of Evidence to Mutiny Enquiry.

66 Thomas Daly and Patrick Sellars [hereafter Daly and Sellars] to Minister Duggan, 18 May 1922 (NAI, D/T, S9048).

67 Evidence of P. Brennan, 21 July 1922, in Minutes of Evidence to Mutiny Enquiry.

68 *Ibid.*

69 *Ibid.*

70 Evidence of Sellars, 15 July 1922, in Minutes of Evidence to Mutiny Enquiry.

71 Evidence of Ring, 14 July 1922, in Minutes of Evidence to Mutiny Enquiry.

72 Evidence of Sergeant Keenan, 14 July 1922, in Minutes of Evidence to Mutiny Enquiry.

73 Evidence of Ring, 14 July 1922, in Minutes of Evidence to Mutiny Enquiry.

74 Evidence of Sergeant Frank Murray, 14 July 1922, in Minutes of

Evidence to Mutiny Enquiry.

75　Evidence of Ring, 14 July 1922, in Minutes of Evidence to Mutiny Enquiry.

76　*Ibid.*

77　Evidence of Superintendent John Keane, 14 July 1922, in Minutes of Evidence to Mutiny Enquiry. The men who withdrew from the depot with Ring were: Deputy Commissioner Patrick Walsh, Chief Superintendents Mathias McCarthy and Michael McCormack, Superintendents James Brennan, Francis Burke, John. J. Byrne, John Galligan, Patrick Harte, John Keane, Jeremiah Maher, Thomas Neary, Bernard O'Connor and Edmond Prendiville (Civic Guard: Subsistence Allowance, D/J 99/15).

78　Daly and Sellars to Duggan, 18 May 1922 (NAI, D/T, S9048).

79　Cross-examination of Sellars by Walsh, 15 July 1922, in Minutes of Evidence to Mutiny Enquiry.

80　Evidence of P. Brennan, 21 July 1922, in Minutes of Evidence to Mutiny Enquiry.

81　*Ibid.*

82　Liddy, 'Smothered History', March 1963, p. 39.

83　*Ibid.*

84　Daly and Sellars to Duggan, 22 May 1922 (NAI, D/T, S9048).

85　P. Brennan, 'Circular to the Officers and Men of the Civic Guard', 22 May 1922 (NAI, D/T, S9048).

86　Evidence of P. Brennan, 21 July 1922, in Minutes of Evidence to Mutiny Enquiry.

87　*Ibid.*

88　Evidence of Sellars, 15 July 1922, in Minutes of Evidence to Mutiny Enquiry.

89　Michael Collins, address to Civic Guard Recruits at Kildare Barracks, 26 May 1922 (GM, Walsh Papers).

90   *Ibid.*

91   Brady, *Guardians of the Peace*, p. 62.

92   Evidence of Sellars, 15 July 1922, in Minutes of Evidence to Mutiny Enquiry.

93   Evidence of Superintendent Martin Lynch [hereafter Evidence of Lynch], 21 July 1922, in Minutes of Evidence to Mutiny Enquiry.

94   Brady, *Guardians of the Peace*, p. 61.

95   'New premises for Civic Guard', *The Irish Times*, 24 May 1922, p. 6.

96   Liddy, 'Smothered History', June 1963, p. 33.

97   *Ibid.*

98   'Civic Guard: Recruiting', *The Irish Times*, 31 May 1922, p. 4.

99   Evidence of Sellars, 15 July 1922, in Minutes of Evidence to Mutiny Enquiry.

100 *Ibid.*

101 *Ibid.*

102 Evidence of Staines, 14 July 1922, in Minutes of Evidence to Mutiny Enquiry.

103 *Ibid.*

104 *Ibid.*

105 Evidence of P. Brennan, 21 July 1922, in Minutes of Evidence to Mutiny Enquiry.

106 Evidence of Liddy, 15 July 1922, in Minutes of Evidence to Mutiny Enquiry.

107 Evidence of Staines, 14 July 1922, in Minutes of Evidence to Mutiny Enquiry.

108 Evidence of Sellars, 15 July 1922, in Minutes of Evidence to Mutiny Enquiry.

109 *Ibid.*

110 Evidence of Staines, 14 July 1922, in Minutes of Evidence to Mutiny Enquiry.

111 *Ibid.*

112 Evidence of Byrne, 14 July 1922, in Minutes of Evidence to Mutiny Enquiry.

113 *Ibid.*

114 Evidence of Sergeant Patrick McAvinia [hereafter Evidence of McAvinia], 14 July 1922, in Minutes of Evidence to Mutiny Enquiry.

115 See Allen, *The Garda Síochána*, p. 23.

116 Evidence of McAvinia, 14 July 1922, in Minutes of Evidence to Mutiny Enquiry.

117 *Ibid.*

118 Evidence of Byrne, 14 July 1922, in Minutes of Evidence to Mutiny Enquiry.

119 Evidence of McAvinia, 14 July 1922, in Minutes of Evidence to Mutiny Enquiry.

120 Evidence of Byrne 14 July 1922, in Minutes of Evidence to Mutiny Enquiry.

121 *Ibid.*

122 Evidence of McNamara, 14 July 1922, in Minutes of Evidence to Mutiny Enquiry.

123 *Ibid.*

124 *Ibid.*

125 Evidence of Byrne, 14 July 1922, in Minutes of Evidence to Mutiny Enquiry.

126 *Ibid.*

127 Evidence of Staines, 14 July 1922, in Minutes of Evidence to Mutiny Enquiry.

128 Evidence of Guard Michael Fallon, 22 July 1922, in Minutes of Evidence to Mutiny Enquiry.

129 Evidence of Lynch, 21 July 1922, in Minutes of Evidence to Mutiny Enquiry.

130 Liddy, 'Smothered History', June 1963, p. 35.

131 Evidence of Lynch, 21 July 1922, in Minutes of Evidence to Mutiny Enquiry.

132 *Ibid.*

133 Liddy, 'Smothered History', June 1963, p. 35.

134 Evidence of Superintendent P. J. Haugh, 22 July 1922, in Minutes of Evidence to Mutiny Enquiry.

135 Evidence of P. Brennan, 21 July 1922, in Minutes of Evidence to Mutiny Enquiry.

136 *Ibid.*

137 Evidence of Sergeant Patrick Doyle [hereafter Evidence of Doyle], 22 July 1922, in Minutes of Evidence to Mutiny Enquiry.

138 *Ibid.*

139 Evidence of P. Brennan, 21 July 1922, in Minutes of Evidence to Mutiny Enquiry.

140 Evidence of Doyle, 22 July 1922, in Minutes of Evidence to Mutiny Enquiry.

141 Evidence of Lynch, 21 July 1922, in Minutes of Evidence to Mutiny Enquiry.

142 Evidence of Liddy, 15 July 1922, in Minutes of Evidence to Mutiny Enquiry.

143 Evidence of Lynch, 21 July 1922, in Minutes of Evidence to Mutiny Enquiry.

144 Evidence of P. Brennan, 21 July 1922, in Minutes of Evidence to Mutiny Enquiry.

145 *Ibid.*

146 Statement of Michael McKenna, June 1922, 'Civic Guard: Cases of Accidental Shootings 1922–24' (NAI, D/J, H99/23).

147 Cutting from *Evening Herald* within file, 'Civic Guard: Cases of Accidental Shootings 1922–24' (NAI, D/J, H99/23).

148 Staines to Duggan, 22 June 1922, 'Civic Guard: Cases of Accidental Shootings 1922–24' (NAI, D/J, H99/23).

149 'Report of Commission of Enquiry into the Civic Guard Following the Mutiny of 1922' [hereafter Mutiny Enquiry], 17 August 1922 (NAI, D/T, S9048), p. 8.

150 Statement issued by recruits at Kildare and Newbridge Barracks to Provisional Government, 24 June 1922, TD (GM, Walsh Papers).

151 *Ibid.*

152 *Ibid.*

153 Duggan to Brennan, 24 June 1922 (GM, Walsh Papers).

154 Staines to Duggan, 28 June 1922 (NAI, D/T, S9048).

155 Evidence of Prendiville, 15 July 1922, in Minutes of Evidence to Mutiny Enquiry.

156 *Ibid.*

157 Donohue, 'Depot Days in Kildare', p. 617.

158 Brennan to Collins, 7 July 1922 (GM, Walsh Papers).

159 Brennan to Collins, 7 July 1922 (NAI, D/T, S9048).

160 G. MacGabainn, Secretary of Department of Finance, to Brennan, 8 July 1922 (NAI, D/T, S9048).

161 Evidence of Staines, 14 July 1922, in Minutes of Evidence to Mutiny Enquiry.

162 Superintendent Daniel Hallinan's 'Report of Railway Hotel Theft and Decampment of Guards', read out by Staines, 14 July 1922, in Minutes of Evidence to Mutiny Enquiry.

163 *Ibid.*

164 *Ibid.*, p. 17.

165 *Ibid.*, p. 18.

166 *Ibid.*, p. 20.

167 *Ibid.*, p. 19.

168 *Ibid.*

4: The Commission of Enquiry

1   In 1920, Kevin O'Shiel was appointed as a Republican judge in County Galway, where he worked together with Staines, who had been appointed as a liaison officer with the Irish Republican Police. See Fergus Campbell, 'The Last Land War? Kevin O'Shiel's Memoir of the Irish Revolution 1916–1921', *Archivium Hibernicum*, Vol. 57, 2003, p. 155.

2   Cabinet Meeting Papers of the Provisional Government, 11 July, 'Mutiny and Commission of Enquiry' (NAI, D/T, S9048).

3   Warrant of Appointment of a Commission of Enquiry into the Civic Guard, signed by Michael Collins, 12 July 1922 (NAI, D/T, S9048).

4   'Report of First Day's Proceedings in the Commission of Enquiry into the Civic Guard', 13 July 1922, (NAI, D/J, 325/329) p. 2.

5   *Ibid.*

6   *Ibid.*, p. 3

7   *Ibid.*, pp. 4–5.

8   *Ibid.*, p. 11.

9   *Ibid.*, p. 12.

10 Evidence of Staines, 14 July 1922, in Minutes of Evidence to Mutiny Enquiry.

11 *Ibid.*

12 *Ibid.*

13 *Ibid.*

14 *Ibid.*

15 *Ibid.*

16 Chairman of the Commission of Enquiry, Kevin O'Shiel, to Staines, 14 July 1922, in Minutes of Evidence to Mutiny Enquiry.

17 Evidence of Staines, 14 July 1922, in Minutes of Evidence to Mutiny Enquiry.

18   Cross-examination of Staines by Guard J. A. O'Connell, 14 July 1922, in Minutes of Evidence to Mutiny Enquiry.

19   *Ibid.*

20   Evidence of J. Brennan, 14 July 1922, in Minutes of Evidence to Mutiny Enquiry.

21   Evidence of Ring, 14 July 1922, in Minutes of Evidence to Mutiny Enquiry.

22   Evidence of O'Connor, 14 July 1922, in Minutes of Evidence to Mutiny Enquiry.

23   *Ibid.*

24   Evidence of Deputy Commissioner Walsh, 15 July 1922, in Minutes of Evidence to Mutiny Enquiry.

25   'Case for the Men', statement read by J. A. O'Connell, 15 July 1922, in Minutes of Evidence to Mutiny Enquiry.

26   *Ibid.*

27   *Ibid.*

28   *Ibid.*

29   *Ibid.*

30   *Ibid.*

31   *Ibid.*

32   *Ibid.*

33   *Ibid.*

34   *Ibid.*

35   *Ibid.*

36   Evidence of Sellars, 15 July 1922, in Minutes of Evidence to Mutiny Enquiry.

37   Staines interrupts cross-examination of Sellars, 15 July 1922, in Minutes of Evidence to Mutiny Enquiry.

38   Walsh cross-examines Sellars, 15 July 1922, in Minutes of Evidence to Mutiny Enquiry.

39   *Ibid.*

40   Evidence of Sellars, 15 July 1922, in Minutes of Evidence to Mutiny Enquiry.

41   Evidence of Superintendent Seán Liddy, 15 July 1922, in Minutes of Evidence to Mutiny Enquiry.

42   Cross-examination of Liddy by Walsh, 15 July 1922, in Minutes of Evidence to Mutiny Enquiry.

43   *Ibid.*

44   *Ibid.*

45   Evidence of O'Meara, 15 July 1922, in Minutes of Evidence to Mutiny Enquiry.

46   *Ibid.*

47   Evidence of Doyle, 17 July 1922, in Minutes of Evidence to Mutiny Enquiry.

48   *Ibid.*

49   *Ibid.*

50   Cross-examination of Doyle by Walsh, 17 July 1922, in Minutes of Evidence to Mutiny Enquiry.

51   *Ibid.*

52   Evidence of Sergeant Patrick Coy [hereafter Coy] 17 July 1922, in Minutes of Evidence to Mutiny Enquiry. On the establishment of the Civic Guard, only recruits were required to take an Oath of Allegiance to the force. As officers were appointed by the force and not 'recruited', they were not obliged to take the oath.

53   Cross-examination of Coy by Walsh, 17 July 1922, in Minutes of Evidence to Mutiny Enquiry.

54   Evidence of McNamara, Commission of Enquiry, 17 July 1922, in Minutes of Evidence to Mutiny Enquiry.

55   Cross-examination of McNamara by Walsh, 17 July 1922, in Minutes of Evidence to Mutiny Enquiry.

56   *Ibid.*

57 O'Shiel to O'Connell, 17 July 1922, in Minutes of Evidence to Mutiny Enquiry.

58 Minutes of Cabinet Meeting on 17 July 1922 (NAI, D/T, S9048).

59 P. Brennan to Collins, 18 July 1922; see Minutes of Special Commission of Enquiry, p. 2.

60 Acting chairman of the Provisional Government, W. T. Cosgrove, to Collins 19 July 1922 (NAI, D/T, S9048).

61 Evidence of P. Brennan, 21 July 1922, in Minutes of Evidence to Mutiny Enquiry.

62 *Ibid.*

63 *Ibid.*

64 *Ibid.*

65 *Ibid.*

66 *Ibid.*

67 *Ibid.*

68 *Ibid.*

69 *Ibid.*

70 Cross-examination of P. Brennan by Walsh, 21 July 1922, in Minutes of Evidence to Mutiny Enquiry.

71 *Ibid.*

72 *Ibid.*

73 *Ibid.*

74 *Ibid.*

75 *Ibid.*

76 *Ibid.*

77 Evidence of P. Brennan, 21 July 1922, in Minutes of Evidence to Mutiny Enquiry.

78 *Ibid.*

79 *Ibid.*

80 *Ibid.*

81 *Ibid.*

82 Cross-examination of P. J. Haugh by Walsh, 22 July 1922, in Minutes of Evidence to Mutiny Enquiry.

83 *Ibid.*

84 O'Shiel to Walsh and O'Connell, 22 July 1922, in Minutes of Evidence to Mutiny Enquiry.

5: Recommendations of the Commission of Enquiry

1 Minutes of Cabinet Meeting, 3 August 1922 (NAI, D/T, S9048).

2 O'Shiel to Assistant Secretary Michael MacDunphy, 3 August 1922 (NAI, D/J, H99/23).

3 Minutes of Cabinet Meeting, 8 August 1922 (NAI, D/T, S9048).

4 'The Last of the RIC. Dublin Castle's New Masters', *The Irish Times*, 18 August 1922, p. 5.

5 'From Today's London Papers: The Royal Irish Constabulary. Last of the Force', Editorial of *The Times*, reprinted in *The Irish Times*, 16 August 1922, p. 7.

6 Mutiny Enquiry, p. 4.

7 *Ibid.*, p. 8.

8 *Ibid.*, p. 10.

9 *Ibid.*

10 *Ibid.*

11 *Ibid.*

12 *Ibid.*, p. 11.

13 *Ibid.*

14 *Ibid.*

15 *Ibid.*

16 *Ibid.*, p. 12.

17 *Ibid.*

18 *Ibid.*, p. 13.

19 *Ibid.*

20 *Ibid.*

21 *Ibid.*, p. 14.

22 Allen, *The Garda Síochána*, p. 46.

23 Mutiny Enquiry, p. 14.

24 *Ibid.*, p. 15.

25 *Ibid.*, p. 16.

26 *Ibid.*, p. 17.

27 *Ibid.*, p. 18.

28 Minutes of Cabinet Meeting, 18 August 1922 (NAI, D/T, S9048).

29 Lee, *Ireland 1912–1985,* p. 63.

30 'The body in Dublin', *The Irish Times*, 24 August 1922, p. 5.

31 Guard Shaun MacManus to O'Shiel, 1 September 1922 (NAI, D/J, H235/329).

32 *Ibid.*, 31 August 1922.

33 See Gregory Allen, *The Garda Síochána*, pp. 55–6.

34 Brady, *Guardians of the Peace*, p. 73.

35 O'Clery, Conor, *Phrases Make History Here* (The O'Brien Press, Dublin, 1986), p. 66.

36 Brady, *Guardians of the Peace*, p. 73.

37 O'Duffy to O'Friel, 12 February 1923, 'Application for admission to Civic Guard' (NAI, D/J, H99/147).

38 O'Duffy to O'Friel, 21 February 1923, *ibid.*

39 McNiffe, *A History of the Garda Síochána*, p. 24.

40 Superintendent James Brennan to O'Duffy, 1 September 1922, 'Hospital for Civic Guard' (NAI, D/J, H99/27).

41 Recollections of Campbell, 11 October 1977 (Shaw Papers).

42 Recollections of Bill Kelly, 11 April 1978 (Shaw Papers).

43 Dr Michael Kenna, September 1922, 'Death of Guard Thomas Bolton: Summary of facts deposed to at Inquest' (NAI, D/J, H99/198).

44 O'Duffy to Minister Kevin O'Higgins, 24 September 1922,

'Cases of Accidental Shootings 1922–24' (NAI, D/J, H99/23).

45 O'Duffy to members of the Civic Guard, 21 September 1922, 'General Orders – Cases of Accidental Shootings' (NAI, D/J, H99/23).

46 O'Duffy to O'Friel, 26 September 1922 (NAI, D/J, H99/23).

47 Inspector William Griffin, DMP, 'Inquest on Body of Private Green', 6 October 1922, in 'Cases of Accidental Shootings' (NAI, D/J, H99/23).

48 O'Friel to O'Duffy, 9 October 1922, 'Scope of Duties Assigned to Civic Guard' (NAI, D/J, H99/49).

49 O'Duffy to O'Friel, 12 October 1922.

50 *Irish Independent*, 13 June 1977, p. 10.

51 'Bomb thrown into barrack', *The Irish Times*, 2 October 1922, p. 4.

52 Recollections of Campbell 1977–8 (Shaw Papers).

53 McNiffe, *A History of the Garda Síochána*, p. 28.

54 Recollections of Patrick McGonagle, 30 September 1977 (Shaw Papers).

55 Recollections of Patrick McInerney, 9 December 1977 (Shaw Papers).

56 Richard Mulcahy (minister for defence) to Kevin O'Higgins (minister for home affairs), 3 September 1922, 'Civic Guard: General Distribution 1922–26' (NAI, D/J, H99/29).

57 O'Duffy to O'Friel, 19 September 1922, 'Civic Guard: General Distribution 1922–26' (NAI, D/J, H99/29).

58 President W. T. Cosgrave, Dáil Éireann Debates, 11 September 1922, Vol. 1, Col. 72.

59 Deputy Cathal O'Shannon, Dáil Éireann Debates, 11 September 1922, Vol. 1, Col. 87.

60 Minister for home affairs, Kevin O'Higgins, Dáil Éireann Debates, 13 September 1922, Vol. 1, Col. 205.

61   Minister for home affairs, Kevin O'Higgins, Dáil Éireann Debates, 29 September 1922, Vol. 1, Col. 956.

62   *Ibid.*

63   'Machinery of Law', *The Irish Times*, 30 September 1922, p. 5.

64   *Irish Independent*, 2 October 1922.

65   Recollections of Donal Colhoun, 16 April 1984 (Shaw Papers).

66   Recollections of John Shaw, September 1977 (Shaw Papers).

67   John Shaw interviewed by Fergus Black, *The Nationalist*, 15 July 1977, p. 7.

68   Staines to O'Higgins, 3 August 1922, 'Resigned and Dismissed RIC in Civic Guard' (NAI, D/J, H99/22).

69   Minister for home affairs, Kevin O'Higgins, *Iris an Gharda*, Vol. 1, No. 1, 26 February 1923.

6: Aftermath

1   Brady, *Guardians of the Peace*, p. 74.

2   Allen, *The Garda Síochána*, p. 57.

3   The Civic Guard was renamed An Garda Síochána following the enactment on 8 August 1923 of the Garda Síochána (Temporary Provisions) Act 1923.

4   See website at http://www.policehistory.com/walsh.html.

5   See Allen, *The Garda Síochána*, p. 57.

6   Brady, *Guardians of the Peace*, p. 72.

7   See Allen, *The Garda Síochána*, p. 48.

Conclusion

1   'Civic Guard Instructions', 9 September 1922, GM, Staines' file. The original quote actually used 'Civic Guard' rather than 'Garda Síochána', but this was updated by the museum/Garda authorities.

BIBLIOGRAPHY

PRIMARY SOURCES

Constabulary Rules, Guides, Regulations and Registers

Chamberlain, Neville, *Standing Rules of the RIC* (Dublin, 1911)

Constabulary List and Directory (Dublin, 1844) (Haliday/No. 1899, Royal Irish Academy)

Constabulary List and Directory (Dublin, 1900)

Depot standing orders (Dublin, 1847)

Drill book compiled for the use of the Royal Irish Constabulary from the infantry drill book, 1905 (Dublin, 1906)

DMP Supernumerary Allocation Register (Kevin Street, Dublin, 1854–1857)

Reed, Andrew, *The Irish Policeman's Manual*, 2nd edn (Dublin, 1883)

— *The Irish Policeman's Manual*, 3rd edn (Dublin, 1887)

— *The Irish Policeman's Manual*, 4th edn (Dublin, 1891)

— *The Irish Constable's Guide*, 5th edn (Dublin, 1907)

RIC Police Code (Dublin, 1909)

Shaw-Kennedy, James, *Standing Rules and Regulations for the Government and Guidance of the Constabulary Force of Ireland* (Dublin, 1837)

Smith, Joseph, *A Hand-book of Police Duties*, 2nd edn (Dublin, 1896)

Garda Síochána Rules, Guides and Regulations

Láimh-Leabhar Dualgas (Dublin, 1923)

Irish Police Code (Dublin, 1925)

Government Reports

First Report of the Commissioners of National Education in Ireland (1834)

Seventh Report of the Commissioners of National Education in Ireland (1840)

Seventeenth Report of the Commissioners of National Education in Ireland (1850)

Twenty-seventh Report of the Commissioners of National Education in Ireland (1860)

Manuscript Material

The National Archives of Ireland, Dublin (NAI)
　　Department of Justice, H series
　　Department of Justice, 4 series
　　Department of the Taoiseach, S files

The National Archives of the United Kingdom, Kew (NAUK)
　　Colonial Office Papers (CO)
　　Home Office Papers

Garda Museum and Archives, Dublin (GM)
　　Civic Guard Examination Papers
　　Civic Guard Routine Orders
　　Commissioner Staines' File
　　Patrick Walsh Papers

Essex Regiment Museum, Chelmsford, Essex
　　Memoirs of Lieutenant Colonel Trollope

University College Dublin Archives
　　Desmond Fitzgerald Papers

Newspapers

Connacht Sentinel, The
Dublin Evening Post, The
Freeman's Journal, The
Irish Independent
Irish News, The
Irish Times, The
Nationalist, The
United Irishman, The

Online Resources

Dáil debates: debates.oireachtas.ie
University of Limerick Law Library: http://library.law.umn.edu/irishlaw

Privately held collection

Shaw Papers held by the Shaw family, Portarlington, County Laois

Published Primary Sources: Books, Journals and Periodicals

Ball, S. (ed.), *A Policeman's Ireland: Recollections of Samuel Waters, RIC* (Cork University Press, Cork, 1999)

Blake, H. A., 'The Irish Police', *The Nineteenth Century*, Vol. IX, No. 48, 1881, pp. 385–96

Breen, D., *My Fight for Irish Freedom* (Anvil Books, Dublin, 1981)

Curtis, R., *The History of the Royal Irish Constabulary* (McGlashan & Gill, London, 1871)

Donohoe, J., 'Depot Days in Kildare', *Garda Review*, July 1948, pp. 615–19

Dunlop, E. (ed.), *Robert Dunlop (RIC) of Clough, County Antrim: Reminiscences (1825–1875) of a Northern Boyhood, Followed by Service in County Longford and County Kildare, before Retirement in Belfast* (Mid-Antrim Historical Group, Ballymena, 1995)

Fennell, T., *The Royal Irish Constabulary: A History and Personal Memoir*, edited by Rosemary Fennell (University College Dublin Press, Dublin, 2003)

Forbes, J., *Memorandums made in Ireland in the Autumn of 1852* (Smith, Elder and Co., London, 1853)

Grattan, H., *The Speeches of the Right Hon. Henry Grattan, in the Irish Parliament and in the Imperial Parliament*, Vol. I (edited by his son) (Longman, Hurst, Rees, Orme and Brown, Dublin, 1822)

Green-Garrow, G., *In the Royal Irish Constabulary* (Blackwood, London, 1908)

Gaughan, J. A. (ed.), *The Memoirs of Constable Jeremiah Mee, RIC* (Mercier Press, Cork, 2012)

Hall, S. C. & Hall, A. M., *Ireland: Its Scenery, Character &c.* (How and Parsons, London, 1841)

Head, F., *A Fortnight in Ireland* (John Murray, London, 1852)

Kohl, J. G., *Ireland* (Harper & Brothers, New York, 1844)

Le Fanu, W. R., *Seventy Years of Irish Life* (Edward Arnold, London, 1893)

Liddy, S., 'Smothered History', *An Síothadóir*, August 1962–June 1963

Lloyd, C. D. C., *Ireland under the Land League: A Narrative of Personal Experience* (Blackwood & Sons, London, 1892)

Macaulay, J., *Ireland in 1872: A Tour of Observation with Remarks on Irish Public Questions* (H. S. King and Co., London, 1873)

Middlemas, K. (ed.), *Thomas Jones' Whitehall Diary, Vol. III, Ireland, 1918–1925* (Oxford University Press, Oxford, 1971)

Neligan, D., *The Spy in the Castle* (MacGibbon & Kee, London, 1968)

O'Duffy, E., 'History of the Garda Síochána', *Garda Review*, March 1929, pp. 329–41

— 'Recruitment of Garda Síochána', *Garda Review*, May 1929, pp. 542–3

— 'Policemen in the Making', *Garda Review*, June 1929, pp. 652–69

— 'Catering for the Garda', *Garda Review*, July 1929, pp. 778–89

— 'Training', *Garda Review*, August 1929, pp. 896–906

— 'Books of Instruction and Reference,' *Garda Review*, September 1929, pp. 1008–19

Shea, P., *Voices and the Sound of Drums: An Irish Autobiography* (Blackstaff Press, Belfast, 1981)

Shaw, J., 'In the Beginning', *Garda Review*, January 1976, pp. 19–23

Sparrow, R., 'The Training of Colonial Police Officers at the RIC Depot, Phoenix Park, Dublin', *The Royal Irish Constabulary Magazine*, Vol. I, No. 4, February 1912, pp. 114–16

Unpublished Reports, etc.

'Civic Guard: Disciplinary Code', NAI, Department of Justice, H99/52, 1922

'Civic Guard – Organisation Committee Report', NAI, Department of Justice, H99, 1922

'Continental Police Systems', NAI, Department of Justice, H99, 1923

Griffin, W., 'Inquest on body of Private Green', NAI, Department of Justice, H99/23, 1922

Lobb, R. P., 'Training of Police Officers of the West and East African Colonies and Protectorates with the Royal Irish Constabulary', NAUK, Colonial Office 879/98/3, 1908

O'Duffy, E., 'Cases of Accidental Shootings', NAI, Department of Justice, H99/23, 1922

O'Shiel, K. & McAuliffe, M., 'Commission of Enquiry: Recommendations for the Future of the Civic Guard', NAI, Department of Justice, H99/23, 1922

'Report on Conditions at Rath Internment Camp, Co. Kildare', NAI, Department of Finance 2/304–6, 1922

'Scope of Duties to be Assigned to Civic Guard', NAI, Department of Justice, H99/49, 1922

Staines, M., 'Resigned and Dismissed RIC in the Civic Guard', NAI, Department of Justice, H99/22, 1922

Vernon, R. V., 'Report on the Training and Organisation of the Royal Irish Constabulary', NAUK, Colonial Office 884/9/3, 1905

SECONDARY SOURCES

Books and Book Chapters

Abbot, R., *Police Casualties in Ireland 1919–1922* (Mercier Press, Cork, 2000)

Akenson, D., *The Irish Education Experiment: The National System of Education in the Nineteenth Century* (Routledge & Kegan Paul, London, 1970)

Allen, G., *The Garda Síochána: Policing Independent Ireland, 1922–1982* (Gill & Macmillan, Dublin, 1999)

Anderson, D. and Killingray, D. (eds), *Policing and Decolonisation* (Manchester University Press, Manchester, 1992)

Bayley, D., 'The Police and Political Development in Europe', in C. Tilly and G. Almond (eds), *The Formation of National States in Western Europe* (Princeton University Press, Princeton, NJ, 1975)

Bennett, R., *The Black and Tans* (Four Square Books, Dublin, 1961)

Berry, H. (ed.), *Statutes and Ordinances and Acts of the Parliament of Ireland* (Alex Thom & Co., Dublin, 1907)

Brady, C., *Guardians of the Peace* (2nd edn) (Prendeville Publishing, Dublin, 2000)

Breathnach, S., *The Irish Police: From Earliest Times to the Present Day* (Anvil Books, Dublin, 1974)

Brennan, M., *The War in Clare, 1911–1921* (Four Courts Press and Irish Academic Press, Dublin, 1980)

Brewer, J. D., *The Royal Irish Constabulary: An Oral History* (Institute of Irish Studies, Belfast, 1990)

Clarke, A., 'The Colonisation of Ulster and the Rebellion of 1641', in T. W. Moody and F. X. Martin (eds), *The Course of Irish History* (Mercier Press, Cork, 1967), pp. 189–203

Coogan, T. P., *The IRA* (HarperCollins, London, 1995)

Coolahan, J., *Irish Education: Its History and Structure* (Institute of Public Administration, Dublin, 1981)

Connolly, S. J. (ed.), *The Oxford Companion to Irish History* (Oxford University Press, Oxford, 1999)

Corcoran, T., *Education Systems in Ireland from the Close of the Middle Ages* (University College Dublin, Department of Education, 1928)

Curran, J. M., *The Birth of the Irish Free State 1921–1923* (The University of Alabama Press, Tuscaloosa, AL, 1980)

Daly, M., *Dublin: The Deposed Capital – A Social and Economic History, 1860–1914* (Cork University Press, Cork, 1984)

— *The Famine in Ireland* (Dublin Historical Association, Dundalk, 1986)

de Búrca, M., *The GAA: A History* (Gill & Macmillan, Dublin, 1999)

de Vere White, T., *Kevin O'Higgins* (Anvil Books, Tralee, 1986)

Dunne, T., *Rebellions: Memoirs, Memory and 1798* (Lilliput, Dublin, 2004)

Fitzpatrick, D., *Politics and Irish Life, 1913–1921* (Gill & Macmillan, Dublin, 1977)

Frame, R., *Colonial Ireland, 1169–1369* (Helicon, Dublin, 1981)

Gilbert, J. T., *Calendar of Ancient Records of Dublin*, Vol. I (Municipal Council, Dublin, 1889)

Herlihy, J., *The Royal Irish Constabulary: A Short History and Genealogical Guide with a Select List of Medal Awards and Casualties* (Four Courts Press, Dublin, 1997)

— *The Dublin Metropolitan Police: A Short History and Genealogical Guide, 1836–1925* (Four Courts Press, Dublin, 2001)

Hickey, D. J. and Doherty, J. E., *A Dictionary of Irish History Since 1800* (Gill & Macmillan, Dublin, 1980)

Holt, E., *Protest in Arms: The Irish Troubles 1916–1923* (Putnam, London, 1960)

Hopkinson, M., *Green Against Green* (Gill & Macmillan, Dublin, 1992)

— *The Irish War of Independence* (Gill & Macmillan, Dublin, 2004)

Hyland, Á. & Milne, K. (eds), *Irish Educational Documents, Vol. 1: Selection of Documents Relating to the History of Irish Education from the Earliest Times to 1922* (Church of Ireland College of Education, Dublin, 1987)

Keogh, D., *Twentieth-Century Ireland* (Gill & Macmillan, Dublin, 1994)

Lee, J. J., *Ireland 1912–1985* (Cambridge University Press, Cambridge, 1990)

Lyons, F. S. L., *Ireland Since the Famine* (Fontana, London, 1980)

Macardle, D., *The Irish Republic* (Irish Press, Dublin, 1951)

MacDonagh, O., *The Modern Nations in Historical Perspective: Ireland* (Prentice-Hall, Upper Saddle River, NJ, 1968)

Maitland, F. W., *Justice and Peace* (Macmillan, London, 1985)

Malcolm, E., *The Irish Policeman, 1822–1922: A Life* (Four Courts Press, Dublin, 2006)

Maxwell, C., *Irish History from Contemporary Sources* (George Allen & Unwin, London, 1923)

McCartney, D., 'From Parnell to Pearse', in T. W. Moody and F. X. Martin (eds), *The Course of Irish History* (Mercier Press, Cork, 1967), pp. 294–312

McColgan, J., *British Policy and the Irish Administration, 1920–22* (George Allen & Unwin, London, 1983)

McCulloch, G. and Richardson, W., *Historical Research in Educational Settings* (Open University Press, Buckingham, 2000)

McManus, A., *The Irish Hedge School and Its Books, 1695–1831* (Four Courts Press, Dublin, 2002)

McNiffe, L., *A History of the Garda Síochána* (Wolfhound Press, Dublin, 1997)

Mitchell, A., *Revolutionary Government in Ireland* (Gill & Macmillan, Dublin, 1995)

Moody, T. W., 'Fenianism, Home Rule and the Land War', in T. W. Moody and F. X. Martin (eds), *The Course of Irish History* (Mercier Press, Cork, 1967), pp. 275–93

Mosse, G. L. (ed.), *Police Forces in History* (Sage Publications, London, 1975)

Ó Catháin, S., *Secondary Education in Ireland* (Talbot Press, Dublin, 1958)

O'Clery, C., *Phrases Make History Here: Century of Irish Political Quotations, 1886–1986* (The O'Brien Press, Dublin, 1986)

O'Farrell, P., *Who's Who in the Irish War of Independence* (Mercier Press, Cork, 1980)

O'Kelly, D., *Salute to the Gardaí: A History of Struggle and Achievement 1922–1958* (Parkside Press, Dublin, 1959)

Osborough, W. N., *The Irish Statutes, 3 Edward II to the Union, A.D. 1310–1800* (Round Hall, Dublin, 1995)

O'Sullivan, D. J., *The Irish Constabularies, 1822–1922: A Century of Policing in Ireland* (Brandon, Dingle, 1999)

— *District Inspector John A. Kearney – The RIC Man Who Befriended Roger Casement* (Trafford Publishing, Bloomington, IN, 2005)

Palmer, S. H., *Police and Protest in England and Ireland, 1780–1850* (Cambridge University Press, Cambridge, 1988)

Pickering, D., *The Statutes At Large From The First Year of K. William and Q. Mary, To The Eighth Year of K. William III*, Vol. IX (Cambridge, 1764)

Robinson, L., *Lady Gregory's Journals* (Putnam, London, 1946)

Townshend, C., *The British Campaign in Ireland, 1919–1921* (Oxford University Press, Oxford, 1975)

— *Political Violence in Ireland* (Clarendon Press, Oxford, 1983)

Wall, M., 'The Age of Penal Laws', in T. W. Moody and F. X. Martin (eds), *The Course of Irish History* (Mercier Press, Cork, 1967), pp. 217–31

Journal Articles

Allen, G., 'Towards a Model Police Service,' *Garda Review*, April 1974, pp. 28–30

— 'The People's Guard', *An Síochâin*, June 1993, pp. 21–7

Boyle, K., 'Police in Ireland before the Union I', *The Irish Jurist*, Vol. VII, 1972, pp. 115–37

— 'Police in Ireland before the Union II', *The Irish Jurist*, Vol. VIII, 1973, pp. 90–116

— 'Police in Ireland before the Union III', *The Irish Jurist*, Vol. XI, 1973, pp. 323–48

Brewer, J. D., 'Max Weber and the Royal Irish Constabulary: A Note on Class and Status', *British Journal of Sociology*, Vol. 40, No. 1, 1989, pp. 82–96

Campbell, Fergus, 'The Last Land War? Kevin O'Shiel's Memoir of the Irish Revolution 1916–1921', *Archivium Hibernicum*, Vol. 57, 2003, pp. 155–200

Donohue, J., 'Depot Days at Kildare', Garda Review, July 1948

Fedorowich, K., 'The Problems of Disbandment: The Royal Irish Constabulary and Imperial Migration, 1919–29', in K. Jeffrey and C. Brady (eds), *Irish Historical Studies*, Vol. XXX, No. 1, 1996, pp. 88–110

Fulham, G. J., 'James Shaw-Kennedy and the Reformation of the Irish Constabulary, 1836–1838', *Éire–Ireland*, Vol. 16, No. 2, 1981, pp. 93–106

Gahan, R., 'The Police of Old Dublin', *Garda Review*, Vol. 15, No. 7, June 1940, pp. 674–7

Irwin, L., 'The Irish Presidency Courts, 1569–1672', *The Irish Jurist*, Vol. XII, 1977, pp. 104–8

Lowe, W. J. and Malcolm, E. L., 'The Domestication of the Royal Irish Constabulary, 1836–1922', *Irish Economic and Social History*, Vol. XIX, 1992, pp. 27–48

Unpublished Theses

Brady, C., 'Police and Government in the Irish Free State 1922–1933', Unpublished MA thesis, University College Dublin, 1977

McNiffe, L., 'The Garda Síochána: A Social and Administrative History, 1922–1952', Unpublished PhD thesis, National University of Ireland, Maynooth, 1994

INDEX